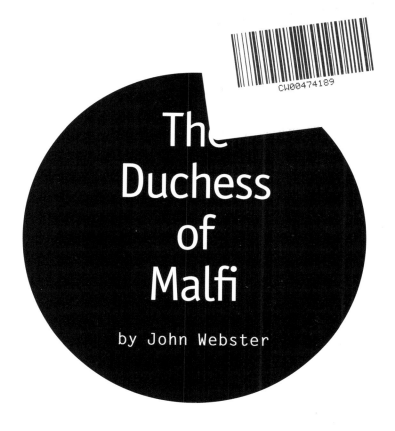

The Duchess of Malfi

by John Webster

Peter Morrisson

Series Editors:
Nicola Onyett and Luke McBratney

HODDER
EDUCATION
AN HACHETTE UK COMPANY

The publisher would like to thank the following for permission to reproduce copyright material:

Acknowledgments:

John Webster: from *The Duchess of Malfi* (1614); **pp. 22 and 31: L. G. Salingar:** from 'The Social Setting', in B. Ford (ed.) *The New Pelican Guide to English Literature, Volume 2: The Age of Shakespeare* (Penguin, 1963); **pp. 32 and 72: Ian Jack:** from 'The case of John Webster', *Scrutiny* (1949); **p.57: T.S. Eliot:** from 'Whispers of Immortality', *Poems* (Hogarth Press, 1918) by permission of Faber & Faber; **pp.30 and 57: Lord David Cecil:** from *Poets and Storytellers* (Constable, 1949); **p.59: Liz Schafer:** from *Times Higher Education* website, www.timeshighereducation.com/features/culture/review-the-duchess-of-malfi/2010517.article (Jan 2014), by permission; **pp.58 and 89: Travis Bogard:** from *The Tragic Satire of John Webster* (University of California Press, 1955); **p.73: Michael Billington:** from *The Guardian*, http://www.theguardian.com/stage/2014/jan/16/the-duchess-of-malfi-review (Jan 2014) Copyright Guardian News & Media Ltd. 2016.

Photo credits:

p.1 © Alinari / REX / Shutterstock; **p.4** © Bettina Strenske / Alamy Stock Photo; **p.5** © Trinity Mirror / Mirrorpix / Alamy Stock Photo; **p.10** © The Granger Collection / TopFoto; **p.12** © Tristram Kenton; **p.47** © TopFoto; **p.55** © Luis Manuel Tapia Bolivar / 123RF.com; **p.65** © World History Archive / Alamy Stock Photo; **p.66** © HIP / TopFoto; **p.67** © TopFoto; **p.70** © The Granger Collection / TopFoto; **p.71** © Roy LANGSTAFF / Alamy Stock Photo; **p.73** © Pete Jones / ArenaPAL / TopFoto

Although every effort has been made to ensure that website addresses are correct at time of going to press, Hodder Education cannot be held responsible for the content of any website mentioned. It is sometimes possible to find a relocated web page by typing in the address of the home page for a website in the URL window of your browser.

Orders: please contact Bookpoint Ltd, 130 Milton Park, Abingdon, Oxon OX14 4SB. Telephone: (44) 01235 827720. Fax: (44) 01235 400454. Lines are open 9.00–17.00, Monday to Saturday, with a 24-hour message answering service. Visit our website at www.hoddereducation.co.uk

© Peter Morrisson, 2016

First published in 2016 by

Hodder Education

An Hachette UK Company,

Carmelite House, 50 Victoria Embankment

London EC4Y 0DZ

Impression number	5	4	3	2	1
Year	2020	2019	2018	2017	2016

Cover photo (and throughout) © Turner-Art / iStockphoto / Thinkstock / Getty Images

Typeset in 11/13pt Bliss Light by Integra Software Services Pvt. Ltd., Pondicherry, India

Printed in Italy

A catalogue record for this title is available from the British Library.

ISBN 9781471854040

Contents

Why read this guide?

The purposes of this A-level Literature Guide are to enable you to organise your thoughts and responses to the text, to deepen your understanding of key features and aspects, and to help you address the particular requirements of examination questions and non-exam assessment (coursework) tasks in order to obtain the best possible grade. It will also prove useful to those of you writing an NEA piece on the text as it provides a number of summaries, lists, analyses and references to help with the content and construction of the assignment.

Note that teachers and examiners are seeking above all else evidence of an *informed personal response to the text*. A guide such as this can help you to understand the text and form your own opinions, and it can suggest areas to think about – but it cannot replace your own ideas and responses as an informed and autonomous reader.

How to make the most of this guide

You may find it useful to read sections of this guide when you need them, rather than reading it through from start to finish. For example, you may find it helpful to read the 'Contexts' section before you start reading the text, or to read the 'Scene summaries and commentaries' section in conjunction with the text – whether to back up your first reading of it at school or college or to help you revise. The sections relating to the Assessment Objectives will be especially useful in the weeks leading up to the exam.

This guide is designed to help you raise your achievement in your examination response to *The Duchess of Malfi*. It is intended for you to use throughout your AS/A-level English literature course. It will help you when you are studying the play for the first time and also during your revision.

The following features have been used throughout this guide to help you focus your understanding of the play:

Context

Context boxes give contextual evidence that relates directly to particular aspects of the text.

Build critical skills

Broaden your thinking about the text by answering the questions in the **Build critical skills** boxes. These help you to consider your own opinions in order to develop your skills of criticism and analysis.

Taking it further ▶▶

Taking it further boxes suggest and provide further background or illuminating parallels to the text.

CRITICAL VIEW

Critical view boxes highlight a particular critical viewpoint that is relevant to an aspect of the main text. This allows you to develop the higher-level skills needed to come up with your own interpretation of a text.

TASK

Tasks are short and focused. They allow you to engage directly with a particular aspect of the text.

Top ten quotation

Top ten quotation

A cross-reference to **Top ten quotations** (see p. 90 of this guide), where each quotation is accompanied by a commentary that shows why it is important.

Since it was first performed in 1614, *The Duchess of Malfi* has been at the centre of a fierce controversy that still rages today. Is it essentially amoral, pessimistic and hopelessly embroiled in despair, *or* is it inspirational, uplifting, transcendent and sublime? Is it simply an over-rated melodrama about a prototypal werewolf driven to distraction by an incestuous desire for his twin sister, *or* is it a profound affirmation of the nobility of the human spirit, which ultimately triumphs in the face of overwhelming adversity? Regarding Webster himself, is he just a thrill-seeking purveyor of gratuitous horror and violence, *or* is he an impassioned moralist primarily motivated by deeply held Christian beliefs? And as for Webster's art, is it merely the crudely assembled borrowings of a literary magpie and shameless plagiarist, *or* is it the product of an outstanding creative genius whose tragic vision is both innovative and unique?

The plague-ravaged world in which the play was conceived was riven between the mental straitjacket of medieval religious theology and the potentially limitless intellectual horizon of the Renaissance quest for understanding. Given the schismatic nature of this environment, is it any wonder that such a maelstrom of mayhem, madness and apparent moral ambiguity should have burst forth upon the stage?

Webster's daring drama tells the tale of a female aristocrat who risks everything for the love of a servant. In defiance of social convention, and her two psychopathic brothers, this quintessentially human heroine boldly challenges a rigidly totalitarian, patriarchal and deeply misogynistic society in order to pursue her own destiny and secretly marry the man she adores. If nothing else, this alone would have split Jacobean audiences into diametrically opposed camps – soft-hearted romantics moved by her passion and courage, and hard-headed traditionalists outraged at her defiance and deceit. But such is the timeless nature of the work that not only does it reflect the desperate plight of women four hundred years ago, it also eloquently speaks for hundreds of millions of women living in many parts of the world today. As Webster has Antonio proclaim in the most poetic of terms, 'She stains the time past, lights the time to come' (I.1).

So, if you like your literature to be relevant and meaningful, as well as explosive and entertaining, and if you relish the prospect of participating in a long-running and still red-hot debate, then at least one thing is for certain – this is the play for you!

NB: All quotations in this guide are cited from the New Mermaid's revised edition, 2014.

The play is set in Italy and opens at the court of the Duchess of Malfi, near Naples, in 1504. Antonio, the man who serves the Duchess of Malfi as Master of her Household, has just returned from France and tells his friend Delio how much he admires the rule of the French King. Bosola enters while they are discussing the merits of the French court; he is clearly unhappy with the way he has been treated by the powerful Cardinal, brother to the Duchess of Malfi. The Cardinal and his brother Ferdinand, the Duchess' twin, are visiting her court.

We hear that Bosola has served a prison sentence for committing a murder for the Cardinal. It is very clear when the Cardinal enters, though, that he has not only failed to reward Bosola for his service, but wants nothing to do with him. From the outset, Bosola appears as the **'malcontent'** in the play. Antonio remarks to Delio that it is a shame that Bosola should be 'thus neglected' as 'This foul melancholy / Will poison all his goodness'. Bosola refuses to be fobbed off by the Cardinal, demanding a reward and stating that he 'will thrive some way'. We hear from Bosola and Antonio of the powerful brothers and their sister, the Duchess of Malfi. The former are both described – not only by Bosola but also by Antonio, who has no personal axe to grind – as utterly corrupt. By contrast Antonio cannot say enough in praise of the Duchess, so much so that Delio accuses him of exaggeration.

The Cardinal wishes to plant a spy in the Duchess' household as he suspects that she, recently widowed, wants to marry again against their interests. Her first husband had been selected by them and she has a child by him, about whom we hear only one mention in the entire play. The Cardinal instructs Ferdinand to hire Bosola as a spy in the Duchess' household, wishing his own hand not to be seen in the affair. Bosola, more eager for status than money, accepts the commission when he is offered the highly prestigious position of Master of the Horse in the Duchess' establishment.

The Duchess has her own plans and, immediately upon her brothers' departure, woos and secretly marries Antonio. Antonio is described by all as noble, accomplished and honourable but, critically, he is a commoner.

In the years that pass, the Duchess has three children by Antonio and, though Bosola discovers the first pregnancy, he ironically suspects Antonio not as the Duchess' partner but as supplying the Duchess in secret with low-born lovers. It does not occur to Bosola or to her brothers that the Duchess might actually have married anyone, let alone Antonio.

Ferdinand finally discovers that she has secretly married someone of low birth and his reaction makes clear his sexual obsession with his sister. The Cardinal agrees that she has **'attainted'** their **'royal blood'** and consequently has the Duchess, Antonio and their children banished, and their property seized by the

▲ Portrait of Doña Isabel de Requesens y Enriquez de Cardona-Anglesola, previously thought to be of Giovanna d'Aragona (1478–1511(?)), the real Duchess of Malfi

Malcontent: a dissatisfied and complaining or rebellious character who was a popular dramatic stereotype of the period. Frequently, this character would rail against social or political injustice. Shakespeare's Hamlet and Iago are famous examples.

Top ten quotation

1

Church and redistributed according to his wishes. His mistress, Julia, obtains some of Antonio's lands.

The Duchess and Antonio split up to increase the chances of saving at least a part of their family, but the Duchess is caught and she and two of their children are arrested. Ferdinand torments the Duchess and finally orders the deaths of her and her children. Bosola oversees these murders as well as that of Cariola, the Duchess' waiting woman. Antonio is unaware of their deaths.

Far from rewarding Bosola, Ferdinand blames him for having killed his 'best friend' and goes mad, whereupon Bosola has an apparent change of heart, swearing to avenge the Duchess and search out and help Antonio. In doing so, he meets Julia, who takes a fancy to him and agrees to draw out the Cardinal, who has pretended to be ignorant of his sister's death. After he has told Julia that it was he who instigated the murders, the Cardinal kills her using a poisoned Bible. Bosola, who has witnessed the whole scene, is once more offered wealth and position by the Cardinal if he agrees to help him cover the tracks of this murder and to find and murder Antonio. He agrees, but his real intention is to save Antonio. The Cardinal then arranges for Bosola to remove Julia's body to her own chambers in the middle of the night, telling everyone at court that they must not stay with Ferdinand during the coming evening and that their attentions towards him are making his madness worse. He tells them they must stay in their own chambers and that he may himself 'feign' some of Ferdinand's 'mad tricks', for example crying out for help, in order to test them.

The Cardinal intends to kill Bosola as soon as the latter has killed Antonio, but Bosola overhears this and, in a tragic mix-up under the cover of darkness, he accidentally kills Antonio, thinking him to be the Cardinal. Bosola then confronts the Cardinal and tells him of his intention to kill him; ironically, the Cardinal's cowardly cries for help are initially ignored by his courtiers. Bosola wounds the Cardinal twice. Ferdinand then enters and in his madness also stabs the Cardinal, at the same time giving Bosola his death wound. In return, Bosola kills Ferdinand. Just before the Cardinal dies, Bosola claims to have avenged the Duchess, Antonio, Julia and himself and, shortly after, he too dies. The play ends with Delio and Pescara, both members of the ruling aristocracy, agreeing

Top ten quotation ⟩ to **'make noble use / Of this great ruin'** by ensuring the only remaining child of the Duchess and Antonio should be acknowledged as the Duchess' legitimate heir.

Target your thinking

- How does Webster develop his themes, settings and characters as the dramatic action unfolds? (**AO1**)
- What dramatic methods does Webster use to shape the audience's responses at crucial points in the play? (**AO2**)

Act I scene 1, lines 1–79

(Note: this section is printed as a separate scene in some editions.)

The entire play covers a period of roughly three to four years of stage time. It opens with Delio welcoming his friend Antonio back from the French court and Antonio then expressing admiration for the 'judicious' French King's rule. They observe the malcontent, Bosola, in conversation with the Cardinal. Bosola complains about the Cardinal's neglect, expressing a bitterly cynical view of courtly reward and service.

Context

The setting is the Duchess' court at Malfi and the play most likely begins in very early 1504, as is suggested by the fact that the horoscope Antonio has drawn up for his and the Duchess' first-born child (in Act II scene 3) is dated December 1504.

Commentary: With Antonio's opening speech, Webster introduces the **Renaissance** motif of the contrast between the ideal and the real world. In so doing, he sets up a model of good government through the description of the French court, suggesting by contrast that, where there is courtly corruption, **'Death and diseases through the whole land spread.'** The rest of the play then powerfully enacts this opening analysis of the effects of corrupt governance, and death and disease dominate both the action and a great deal of the imagery. In terms of action, there are plenty of fatalities lined up for later as the play approaches its tragic denouement and, as for disease, the main sickness appears to be of the mind. Ferdinand increasingly slides into madness and arranges for a demented spectrum of society to torment the Duchess. But there is also an overall sense of a world gone insane and fallen into chaos owing to the self-seeking and self-destructive nature of the political elite.

(For more on what Antonio refers to as 'the corruption of the times' (I.1), see the section on King James' court in the 'Contexts' chapter, p. 65.)

The Renaissance: the period of European history between the fourteenth and seventeenth centuries, in which great advances were achieved in science, technology, philosophy, literature, architecture, and art owing to a renewed interest in the art, literature and architecture of Ancient Greece and Rome. There was also considerable expansion in business, commerce and international exploration.

> Top ten quotation

TASK

Antonio's opening speech sets up the Renaissance motif of the contrast between the ideal and the real world. In what ways does the reality of Act I fall short of Antonio's ideal?

Taking it further ▶

Search the internet for 'King James' favourites' in order to gain an impression of the resentment caused by James' preferment of young Scottish courtiers.

One significant feature of Bosola's dialogue in his conversation with the Cardinal is his use of imagery, which includes 'standing pools' (a striking contrast to Antonio's image of the free-flowing fountain to represent a moral court), demonic possession, physical disability, crowded hospitals, and rapacious and predatory animals. Webster is creating an oppressive atmosphere through the use of disturbing imagery patterns, which will be revisited throughout the play.

Build critical skills

Why is Webster's image of stagnant water so appropriate for characterising a corrupt court? Offer a detailed explanation.

Build critical skills

Why is it necessary for Webster to establish Antonio's worth so early in the play by immediately introducing him as an able horseman and jouster, and as such an astute judge of character?

Act I scene 1, line 80 onwards

Webster's main source for *The Duchess of Malfi* was William Painter's *The Palace of Pleasure*. In keeping with this text, Webster's Antonio is a skilled soldier who has earlier triumphed in a jousting competition. Antonio gives Delio highly accurate character sketches of the moral corruption of the Cardinal and Ferdinand. Of the Duchess, however, he is full of praise. At the Cardinal's instigation, Ferdinand persuades the Duchess to give Bosola the socially prestigious post of Provisor of the Horse in return for spying on behalf of the brothers. The Duchess' brothers urge her never to remarry, and she seems to agree. Left alone with Cariola, she makes it clear she is already intent on remarriage and goes on to woo and marry Antonio in a private ceremony witnessed only by Cariola.

Build critical skills

Why does Webster provide the audience with these character studies of the main characters rather than simply allowing them to reveal themselves more naturalistically through their actions and dialogue?

▲ Ferdinand and the Cardinal urge the Duchess not to remarry, taken from Dominic Dromgoole's 2014 production of the play staged at the Sam Wanamaker Playhouse and starring Gemma Arterton as the Duchess, David Dawson as Ferdinand and James Garnon as the Cardinal

Commentary: During the first half of Act I, Webster uses Antonio, and to a lesser extent Delio, to provide extremely unflattering character studies of Bosola, the Cardinal and Ferdinand. Bosola immediately conforms to the dramatic stereotype of the malcontent: bitter, disaffected and railing at courtly corruption largely on account of his own failure to achieve worldly success.

As Antonio suggests, Ferdinand is volatile and unpredictable, whereas the Cardinal is more circumspect in his political manipulations, thus representing another theatrical stereotype of the revenge tragedy genre, the machiavel. His language is far more restrained than Ferdinand's, as is illustrated when the brothers urge their sister not to remarry. Ferdinand's imagery reeks of sexual innuendo: 'most luxurious' (lustful), 'Whores, by that rule…', 'rank pasture', 'honey-dew', 'a neat knave with a smooth tale' and 'Farewell, lusty widow'. The Cardinal, in contrast, uses abstract nouns such as 'discretion', 'honour' and 'wisdom'. Webster's choice of language suggests their differing motivations for desiring that the Duchess should not remarry: the Cardinal is concerned with family prestige and his own social standing, whereas Ferdinand is clearly preoccupied with his twin sister's sexuality. Webster creates considerable dramatic impact via these very different characterisations of the Duchess' brothers.

Dramatic interest is also created by the fact that Webster keeps the Duchess in the background on her first entrance. We hear about her from the point of view of Antonio, who presents her as almost divine, the role model for 'all sweet ladies'. As the scene progresses, the Duchess takes centre stage. Assailed by her brothers' demands that she should not remarry, she responds with wit and spirit, but does appear to make an explicit promise to follow their advice. She says, 'Will you hear me? / I'll never marry.' When Ferdinand exits, however, she states her determination to disobey her brothers' orders, aware that she is embarking on a 'dangerous venture'.

At first glance, Bosola may appear to be no more than a villainous instrument of the brothers' sinister plans, but in fact his character is complex and ambiguous. Initially, he rejects the gold offered by Ferdinand, saying that he is unprepared to risk his soul to become an 'intelligencer' (a spy), but he accepts the corrupt employment when he learns of the post as Provisor of the Horse that Ferdinand has secured for him in the Duchess' household. It would therefore seem that social status, rather than money, is Bosola's main motivation. In this way, Webster uses Bosola to make a powerful comment about the corrupting influence of a society that fails to provide honest opportunities for ambition and talent.

▲ Helen Mirren as the Duchess at The Roundhouse, London, 1981

Taking it further ▶▶

In order to understand the significance of Ferdinand's offer to Bosola, use the internet to search for 'the royal office of Master of the Horse'.

Build critical skills

How accurate is Antonio's analysis that Bosola's 'foul melancholy', which arises out of being 'neglected', is the root cause that 'Will poison all his goodness...'? Can you apply a psychological reading to this?

The climax of the scene is the Duchess' wooing of Antonio. Powerful and moving, Webster creates a refreshing delicacy here, which starkly contrasts with the blatant menace and tension of the earlier conversation between the Duchess and her two brothers. Webster shows a deftness and subtlety when conveying Antonio's surprise and the Duchess' initial tentativeness as she reverses the conventional gender roles. But a breathtaking momentum is maintained owing to the speed at which the Duchess guides Antonio through the stages of wooing, wedding and bedding.

This wooing sequence is extremely impressive in its humanity and is one of the high points of the play. We are shown two people whose powerful mutual attraction is forced to operate under the restrictions of unsympathetic social expectations. The attempt of the Duchess and Antonio to find happiness and fulfilment through a loving marriage may well be socially forbidden, but Webster certainly presents it as an entirely wholesome expression of human sexuality. This is in stark contrast to the attitudes to sex of her two brothers, as revealed later in the play: the Cardinal's gloating participation in the cuckoldry of Julia's husband, Castruchio, and Ferdinand's unhealthily obsessive desire with his sister's body. In particular, the gentle sexual intimation used by the Duchess, 'Lay a naked sword between us, keep us chaste', provides a refreshing contrast to the blatantly crude innuendo used by Ferdinand earlier in the scene: 'What cannot a neat knave with a smooth tale / Make a woman believe?'

TASK

Re-read the Duchess' wooing of Antonio and make a note of the ways in which Webster's extremely delicate use of language evokes the passion, vulnerability, empathy and humanity of the Duchess, thus genuinely convincing us that she is indeed 'flesh and blood'.

Context

Webster may well be using Castruchio to satiate the general public's dissatisfaction with the quality of King James' courtiers, who were frequently regarded as foolish, foppish and unmanly. (See the section on King James' court in 'Contexts', p. 65.)

Build critical skills

The Duchess' secret marriage is conducted without the blessing of the Church and her bold defiance of convention is embodied in her comment that 'We now are man and wife, and 'tis the Church / That must but echo this.' How might Webster's contemporary audience have reacted to such individualism?

Act II scene 1

It is now December 1504 and the setting is still the Duchess' court at Malfi. Bosola engages in insulting banter with Castruchio and an Old Lady, in which he satirises courtly ambition and female vanity. Bosola suspects that the Duchess is pregnant and plans to give her apricots to prove this. Antonio tells Delio that he and the Duchess are married. Bosola offers the Duchess apricots, which set off her labour. Delio urges the dazed Antonio to put into action his plans for the Duchess' confinement and to excuse her isolation by suggesting that the apricots were poisoned and that she does not trust any doctors to treat her.

Commentary: The scene begins by reintroducing the central theme of ambition, which – through Antonio's words in the previous scene – has already been established as 'a great man's madness'. In terms of both the play and Jacobean society, one of the key focuses of ambition was to rise at court, thus reflecting the often ruthless competitiveness of King James' own courtiers. (See the section on King James' court in 'Contexts', p. 65.) Here, however, the tone is obviously **satirical**, as Bosola instructs Castruchio on how to fulfil his ambition of being 'an eminent courtier' through such ludicrous acts as twirling 'the strings of your band with a good grace' and blowing your nose at the end of a sentence. Of course, as Bosola dutifully adds, this also involves a morally questionable measure of deliberate deception, such as giving false hope to a prisoner whom you intend to condemn to be hanged by firstly smiling upon him.

> **Satire:** the use of humour to mock vice, stupidity, misuse of power, etc.

Context

In *A Courtier*, his satirical characterisation of courtiers, Sir Thomas Overbury declares, 'He puts more confidence in his words than meaning, and more in his pronunciation than his words.' Tragically, Overbury died of poisoning in the Tower of London in 1613, having been imprisoned by King James as a result of his opposition to the forthcoming marriage of Frances Howard to Robert Carr, a highly influential courtier and King James' favourite. (See the section on King James' court in 'Contexts', p.65.)

> **Build critical skills**
>
> Ambition is frequently a cause of concern in Renaissance literature. In what ways is it being presented here as an undesirable trait?

Bosola's dialogue changes from prose to blank verse, presumably to reflect the more serious tone as his gruesome images of disease and rottenness highlight another of the play's serious themes, the corporeal nature of man. This is also one of the major themes of the Bible – that life is short and God's judgement is inevitable, so good conduct is essential for one's ultimate spiritual welfare. (For more on this, see the *Ephemeral nature of man* section in 'Themes', p. 33.)

Having used Bosola yet again to progress the theological and moral subtext, Webster once more develops Bosola's role as a prime mover in terms of the action. Bosola intends to test his suspicions about the Duchess being pregnant by tempting her with apricots, a fruit commonly believed to induce labour.

Note that it is Delio who takes charge of the crisis of the Duchess' premature labour, while Antonio is 'lost in amazement'.

Act II scene 2

Bosola offers further insults to the Old Lady. Antonio orders the palace gates to be locked and summons the court staff. He tells them the Duchess is sick in her room but that someone has stolen her jewellery and money. Left alone with Delio, Antonio expresses his and the Duchess' anxiety. Cariola tells Antonio that the Duchess has given birth to a son and so Antonio leaves to draw up the child's horoscope.

> **Context**
>
> Most Jacobeans believed that the alignment of such celestial bodies as stars and planets at the exact time of a child's birth could be used to predict that child's future. In general, this popular mystical belief in astrology did not appear to conflict with their Christian religious convictions.

Commentary: This is a bustling, night-time scene of activity and suspense as Bosola's attempts to discover the truth about the Duchess are thwarted by Antonio's ploy of a robbery for concealing the birth of their child. At times, the tension is undercut by the distasteful sexual innuendo of both Bosola, in his talk of lust and pregnancy, and the servants, in their discussion of the supposed intruder: 'With a pistol in his great codpiece!' Delio remains cool and reliable. He is dismissive of Antonio's superstitious fears, setting himself up as a man of practical common sense.

Act II scene 3

Prowling the palace that night, Bosola hears a woman's screams before bumping into Antonio. Antonio makes the excuse that he was drawing up a horoscope for tracing the Duchess' stolen jewels, then he demands to know why Bosola is abroad. He suggests that the apricots Bosola gave the Duchess were poisoned, and insinuates that Bosola might have been involved in the robbery. Antonio has a nosebleed and accidentally drops the child's horoscope. Denying Bosola access to the Duchess' chamber and insisting that Bosola clear his name in the morning, Antonio leaves. Bosola reads the horoscope, which confirms the child's birth, and suggests that 'Time will discover' the father. Meanwhile, he makes plans to send the news to the Duchess' brothers in Rome via Castruchio, who is due to travel there the next day.

Commentary: The tension here is heightened by the night-time setting, the offstage noises and 'the rising of the wind', which suggests a gathering storm. This all helps to intensify the onstage antagonism between Antonio and Bosola, giving an additional edginess to their dialogue that is further enhanced by Antonio's anxious asides to the audience, e.g. 'This fellow will undo me'.

Props are significant. The reference to Bosola's 'dark lantern' is a Jacobean convention to signify a night-time setting, whether in daylight performances at the Globe or candlelit ones at Blackfriars. The horoscope and handkerchief that Antonio drops are particularly important, and the latter, with Antonio's embroidered initials soaked in his nasal blood, provides a sinister premonition of his death. Ominous, too, is the horoscope's prediction of a 'short life' and 'violent death' for the new-born child. The audience might remember this at the end of the play, when the same child is presented by Delio as the Duchess' 'hopeful' heir.

Act II scene 4

In Rome, the Cardinal is entertaining his mistress, Julia, who is old Castruchio's wife. Castruchio arrives, as does Delio, one of Julia's former suitors. Delio offers Julia money to become his mistress but she rejects him. The servant announces that Ferdinand has responded passionately to a letter delivered to him by Castruchio and Delio reflects on the possibility that Antonio's secret has been discovered.

Commentary: The Cardinal's conversation with Julia advances the theme of blatant misogyny already witnessed in earlier scenes (mainly from Bosola's insults to the Old Lady), as he offends her with his accusations about women's lack of constancy. This is immediately followed by Delio's propositioning of her, which reduces her to the level of a prostitute. This adds to the general impression of women continually being demeaned by men, while simultaneously deepening the play's presentation of moral ambiguity. Webster has tarnished Delio and thus may have subtly diminished the sense of virtue that is attached to him.

This scene is dramatically useful in that it allows Webster to introduce a deliberate delay to the main action, which is clearly threatening to gather pace as a result of Castruchio's arrival in Rome with Bosola's report. The corrupt nature of the adulterous relationship between Julia and the Cardinal, coupled with the obvious lack of warmth, also acts as a powerful contrast to the genuine love and affection that we see between Antonio and the Duchess at the end of Act I, and consequently serves to invest their relationship with a greater degree of moral legitimacy.

Act II scene 5

Ferdinand shares the news about the Duchess' child with the Cardinal, speculating on the identity of the father and threatening violent revenge.

Commentary: Volatile and unstable, Ferdinand has been thrown into a violent passion by Bosola's news of the birth of the child. He says he has 'grown mad', and his mental imbalance develops from this point to its climax into **lycanthropia** after the Duchess' death in Act IV. His fury is motivated in part by incestuous sexual jealousy, yet he also takes a perverse delight in imagining his sister in 'the shameful act of sin' with various lovers of low social status. Ferdinand's urge towards sexually sadistic revenge is just as unrestrained as his sexual fantasising, culminating in the threat to feed the Duchess' lover a broth made from their child.

> **Build critical skills**
>
> It may be argued that Delio's motives are actually pure, in that he wishes to cultivate Julia only in order to gain inside information about the Cardinal's plans and so protect Antonio. What do you think?

> Lycanthropia: imagining oneself to be a wolf.

CRITICAL VIEW

A modern psychological reading may well see Ferdinand's lycanthropia on a Freudian level, i.e. as a manifestation of a deep-rooted sexual problem. Commenting on the depiction of the werewolf in today's culture, Phillip A. Bernhardt-House states: 'The schizophrenia of so many modern werewolves is a symptom, perhaps, of the rather poor relationship a great deal of human society has with sexuality – its most animal and bestial set of behaviours' ('The Werewolf as Queer, the Queer as Werewolf, and Queer Werewolves', *Queering the Non/human*, 2008).

▲ A fifteenth-century engraving of a werewolf attacking a victim

The scene is made even more interesting because this is the first time that we can fully appreciate the contrasting personalities of the two brothers. The Cardinal, though just as angry at their sister for having **'attainted'** their **'royal blood'** through her low union, remains restrained and eventually becomes disgusted by Ferdinand's intemperance. He astutely recognises Ferdinand's imminent madness and urges him to regain his self-control. To the Cardinal, such passion reduces men to beastliness and deformity and exceeds all 'reason'.

Top ten quotation

Act III scene 1

The action returns to Malfi and a period of approximately two years has elapsed since the previous scene, as is indicated by the fact that in the intervening time the Duchess has given birth to two more children. Antonio is worried that news of his growing family has reached the Cardinal and Ferdinand, as the latter has recently arrived at court and is behaving with ominous restraint. Ferdinand suggests Count Malateste as a potential husband for the Duchess and tells Bosola of his intention to extract the truth from his sister about the father of her children that night, planning to do this by use of a key to her bedchamber that Bosola has recently acquired.

Commentary: It might seem unlikely that nothing has come of Ferdinand's violent threats during the time that has elapsed since the previous scene, but in this Webster is once again following Painter's lead by delaying the Aragonian brothers' revenge until they have discovered the identity of the father of the Duchess' children. Webster guides our acceptance of such a sudden passage of time through the light-hearted way he has Delio remind us that we are observing a play: 'Methinks 'twas yesterday / …verily I should dream / It were within this half hour.'

Antonio relates to Delio the scandalous reports that are common currency among the people, according to which the Duchess is regarded as a 'strumpet'. Of equal concern is the belief that Antonio is embezzling great sums of money. Again following Painter's lead, Webster may well be indicating how the Duchess' marriage for love is in conflict with her duties. Ferdinand seems to have taken his brother's advice to heart and has himself well under control. Antonio is sceptical about his quietness but the Duchess seems anxious to gain her brother's good opinion, though she dismisses his choice of Count Malateste (a name suggestive of sexual impotency in its implication of malfunctioning male genitalia) as a suitor and is forced into open deception in promising that when she marries it will be to Ferdinand's honour. She is open with him about the scandalous reports of her and seems genuinely relieved and grateful when he responds with what appears to be love and consideration.

Ferdinand's true feelings, however, emerge in elements of his language when in conversation with Bosola, especially his reference to 'the witchcraft [that] lies in her rank blood', which appears to be a tacit acknowledgement of the torment he experiences as a result of his inability to resist his unnatural obsession with his sister's body. He has, however, been able to cling on to his sanity thus far.

Bosola, meanwhile, is playing the part of the loyal servant and spy, talking almost in his master's voice about the Duchess' 'bastards', but does he really believe what he says about witchcraft and love potions? His apparent belief in sorcery sits oddly with his sarcasm at Ferdinand's suggestion that 'all things are written' in the stars. The answer may well be that Bosola is simply not so much a creature of contradiction as a contrary creature who is driven to antagonism, even to the extent of challenging his social superiors. By the end of the play, however, his dialogue suggests a powerful conviction in the workings of fate.

Build critical skills

Webster uses a great deal of theatrical imagery. Why do you think he does this?

Build critical skills

If Bosola's main motivation for the controversial assertions he frequently makes is one of contrariness towards others, can we really trust anything that he says?

Build critical skills

Bosola has been employed to spy on the Duchess and yet three years and three children later, he has learned virtually nothing. Is he not much of a spy? Or is Bosola deliberately extending his work to ensure he keeps his money-spinning job going?

Context

```
The conversation about the efficacy of love potions in this
scene may well be an allusion to Frances Howard's alleged
use of them in her successful attempt to ensnare King
James' favourite, Robert Carr. This came out during the Sir
Thomas Overbury murder trials. (See the King James' court
section in the 'Contexts' chapter, p.65.)
```

Act III scene 2

Ferdinand comes to the Duchess' bedroom and discovers she is married. He sets out for Rome on horseback. The Duchess hastens Antonio's flight to Ancona by publicly dismissing him from her service and confiscating his money and possessions. Bosola tricks the Duchess into telling him that Antonio is her husband and she puts him in charge of her affairs, sends him after Antonio, and accepts his suggestion that she should feign a pilgrimage to Loreto rather than join Antonio directly. Cariola is uneasy and suggests an alternative strategy, but the Duchess calls her a 'superstitious fool'.

Commentary: The relaxed domesticity in the first part of the scene provides a powerful dramatic contrast to the tension that immediately ensues on Ferdinand's unexpected entrance. The light sexual banter between the Duchess and Antonio suggests a warmth and intimacy that is far removed from the distasteful sexual innuendo and aggressive misogyny that the audience observed the Cardinal direct towards Julia in Act II scene 4.

Although Antonio is often seen as a dull and ineffective character, here he easily matches the sparkling repartee of the women, and much of his attractiveness to the Duchess is clearly demonstrated to be that, in contrast to most men of the time, he is quite simply a man who enjoys the company of women. His contributions are full of a lively sense of fun: for example his tongue-in-cheek response to Cariola's double entendre about him always 'rising' so early when he sleeps with the Duchess, in which he playfully refers to the chores of 'Labouring men'. Later in the scene, however, Antonio again exhibits weakness when he reappears only after Ferdinand's departure, blames and then threatens to shoot Cariola for Ferdinand's incursion, and flounders as his wife takes control in the sudden emergency. But he plays his role well in the ruse of the false accusation levelled against him, even managing to frame words that secretly convey his love and commitment to the Duchess in the guise of a formal self-defence. He departs with considerable dignity.

▲ Ferdinand threatens the Duchess with a poniard, from the Old Vic production, May 2012

The Duchess herself is revealed at her best and worst in this scene. With her husband she is loving, witty and human; in the face of her brother's violent accusations she shows courage and spirit (**'Why might not I marry? / I have not gone about in this to create / Any new world or custom'**); and she is both authoritative and resourceful in the way she deals with the emergency. Yet her secret marriage has led her into dishonesty and deception and has now

Top ten quotation

destabilised her entire court ('**Oh misery, methinks unjust actions / Should wear these masks and curtains, and not we…**'); her trust in Bosola is naive and gullible; and her overruling of Cariola's alternative suggestion for a secular pretext to her journey is ungrateful, arrogant and potentially sacrilegious. Her 'worst' is not really so bad, however, and certainly helps to make her a touching, human and believable character. The **protagonist**'s human fallibility is at the heart of all great tragedy.

◁ Top ten quotation

Protagonist: the principal character.

Act III scene 3

The Cardinal discusses with Count Malateste the military situation that requires them both to 'turn soldier'. Webster makes clear that although the Cardinal was a skilled military man prior to his entry into the Church, Malateste merely pretends at it. The Marquis of Pescara and the other lords observe the reactions of Ferdinand and the Cardinal to the news that Bosola brings. Attention shifts to the brothers, who react with anger at the unmasking of Antonio as their sister's husband and to her feigned pilgrimage to Loreto. The brothers begin to lay plans to thwart the pair's escape.

Commentary: The Cardinal's prospective transformation into a soldier is another ironic reminder of the worldliness of this supposed spiritual leader and of the hypocrisy of the Catholic Church in its quest for temporal power. This transition to a war footing also foreshadows the impending bloodshed of later events.

Build critical skills

To what extent do you consider the intrusiveness of the ongoing character studies an asset or a hindrance to the dramatic impact of the play?

The further character study that Webster provides in this section for Bosola, this time via Delio, is rather odd. When we think of everything Delio could have said about Bosola, including his shady past, it seems at first strange that he merely offers an anecdote about Bosola's reputation in his student days. The key words, however, are that he studied fanatically in order to 'gain the name of a speculative man', Bosola's central drive being societal recognition.

This scene closes with a shift of focus back to Ferdinand and the Cardinal, the former typically obsessed with the Duchess' 'beauty' and sexual betrayal, the latter hypocritically sanctimonious in his disgust at the Duchess making 'religion her riding-hood'. Ferdinand expresses his intention to write to the Duchess' son by her first husband, the official heir to the dukedom, as a first step in restoring what he, and many of Webster's audience, would have regarded as the correct social order. This young man is not mentioned again in the play, but it is worth remembering that he is not the one promoted by Delio **'in's mother's right'** at the end of the play.

◁ Top ten quotation

Act III scene 4

Two pilgrims at the shrine of Our Lady of Loreto observe the Cardinal's investiture as a soldier, followed immediately by the banishment of the Duchess and her entire family, during which the Cardinal violently removes her wedding ring. The pilgrims comment on these events, questioning the legitimacy of the state of Ancona to banish 'a free prince' and the Pope's seizure of the duchy of Malfi. The pilgrims are sympathetic to the Duchess and Antonio, though surprised at her choice of low-born husband, and they predict Antonio's downfall.

Context

Once again, Webster portrays the Roman Church as being far too concerned with temporal power and wealth. (See the Religion section in the 'Contexts' chapter, p.71.)

TASK

What does the sycophantic 'ditty' sung in praise of the Cardinal suggest about his character? In what ways does this false impression clash with what we know to be the truth about him?

Commentary: This scene employs two features of Jacobean dramaturgy – chorus and dumb show – that may seem odd to us today. In dumb shows, a key moment of the narrative is acted out in mime and visual display, usually accompanied by music. Dramatists of the period used them sparingly, but effectively, at points where narrative and action are more important than character and psychology. The device of the chorus, represented here by the two pilgrims, derives from Greek tragedy, where groups of anonymous characters, often speaking in unison, provide essential background information or comment on the play's action. In this scene, the enormity of the event dwarfs the Duchess and her family and thus suggests the overwhelming nature of the forces opposed against them: the Church, the state and the political power of her highly influential brothers.

Webster's two pilgrims offer an objective response to what is enacted in the dumb show. The audience trusts the pilgrims because of their simple religious status and the fact that they are separate from the central events of the plot, being observers rather than participants. The pilgrims recognise the Duchess' faults, her socially unequal marriage and her 'looseness'. Again, Webster makes clear how much the Duchess' defiance of social propriety has undermined her authority and standing in the world. He also, however, exhibits considerable sympathy for the Duchess through the First Pilgrim's remark about the Cardinal's 'cruel' treatment of her and through the two pilgrims' joint questioning of the legality of the Pope's seizure of the Duchess' lands. Through them, Webster also challenges social convention and thus differs markedly from his main source, William Painter.

Act III scene 5

The Duchess and Antonio, with their family and remaining household servants, discuss their situation. Antonio interprets a dream the Duchess has had. Bosola brings a letter from Ferdinand apparently proposing reconciliation, but the offer is rejected. The family splits up after Bosola leaves, Antonio taking the eldest son away with him and intending to head for Milan. Bosola returns with armed men and the Duchess is arrested.

Commentary: As in Painter's version of the tale, the Duchess' changed fortunes are emphasised by the shrinking of her household to 'this poor remainder'. Through Antonio, Webster once more warns against the employment of flatterers: 'From decayed fortunes every flatterer shrinks…' Antonio may again seem largely ineffectual in allowing his wife to make the decisions and far from the man of action suggested by his triumphant participation in the jousting at the start of the play. As unmanly as his departure might seem, however, as he flees with his eldest son and leaves the Duchess and his other two children to certain captivity, Webster is once more following Painter's lead.

Webster's skilful characterisation of the Duchess yet again displays a variety of qualities that give her a touching humanity. She is anxious about the interpretation of her dream, resentful of her brothers' power over her and rightly sceptical of Ferdinand's message, which is loaded with frequent equivocation: 'I want his head in a business'. Despite her extreme trepidation, she is loving towards her husband and children, resourceful and practical in planning the escape of Antonio and their eldest son, and shows tremendous courage and dignity when she herself is taken.

Bosola's contempt for Antonio's low social status is evident here: he sarcastically refers to his 'breeding' to his face, and denigrates him to the Duchess as 'this base, low fellow', and 'One of no birth'. However, this is not necessarily to be taken literally. We have to remember that Bosola also springs from 'base' roots in terms of birth and thus, as with so many of Bosola's statements perhaps, once again, his deeply antagonistic nature is merely revelling in being contrary. Interestingly, Webster qualifies Bosola's prejudice – and its inherent justification of a social order that places value on a person largely as a result of class – with the Duchess' seditious dog-fish parable as she is arrested, which argues that hierarchical position is no true indicator of human merit.

Act IV scene 1

The Duchess – now under arrest – is visited in darkness by Ferdinand, who offers her a dead man's hand, pretending at first that it is his. He then walks away, leaving her holding it and implying that it is Antonio's. Antonio's dead body, with that of their children, is now revealed to her, though we later learn that these are merely wax figures. In despair, the Duchess longs for death. Bosola urges Ferdinand to end his cruelty, but Ferdinand intends to continue the emotional torment by plaguing the Duchess with the lunatics from the local asylum. Ferdinand vows revenge on Antonio.

Commentary: The location for this scene is unclear. Bosola had informed the Duchess in the previous scene that she was to be transported 'To your palace' in Malfi. As in Painter's version of the story, however, it would appear that this assurance was false and that instead she has actually been taken to some bleak prison. Although the Duchess' death scene in Painter's version is graphic and cruel, Webster greatly intensifies and prolongs the horror with the protracted psychological torture elements that he introduces. Scenes such as this give Jacobean tragedy its reputation for grotesque melodrama, but much more important here is the Duchess' heroic response to the cruelty inflicted upon her, which enables Webster to elevate her to true tragic grandeur.

On the other hand, Ferdinand is infinitely inferior in all senses, apart from raw power. His cruelty, his relish of his appalling tricks, his obsessive jealousy and his determination to reduce his sister to despair, all fully expose his psychopathy. He is even resentful of the Duchess' fortitude, which, in Bosola's words, demonstrates 'a behaviour so noble / As gives a majesty to adversity'. Even Bosola seems genuinely impressed by her stoicism but, equally, given his perversity, he could deliberately be trying to antagonise Ferdinand.

The naming of an (imaginary) artist, Vincentio Lauriola, as being commissioned by Ferdinand to create the stage device of the waxworks helps create a shocking semblance of reality to what is essentially a moment of gross theatrical

> **Build critical skills**
>
> What possible interpretations might there be of the Duchess' impassioned declaration mid-scene, 'And yet, oh heaven, thy heavy hand is in't'?

Taking it further ▶

Explore other contemporary uses of stage imagery by searching online for 'theatre as metaphor in Shakespeare'.

> Top ten quotation

The Fourth Wall: an imaginary 'wall' at the front of the stage through which the audience observes the action.

Antimasque: a comic or grotesque dance presented before or between the acts of a masque.

sensationalism. When presented with the waxwork tableau, the Duchess temporarily succumbs to the despair that Ferdinand wishes on her, craving death and taking refuge in curses. Whatever her perceived faults might be, an audience cannot fail to be moved by the all-too-human torment that brings her to the verge of a complete loss of faith.

The Duchess' comment that 'I account this world a tedious theatre, / For I do play a part in't 'gainst my will' appears daring in the sense that Webster runs the risk of undermining the tension he has created by having the Duchess breach **the Fourth Wall**, thus reminding the audience that they are watching a play. Such theatrical imagery, however, is a regular feature in the drama of the period. Furthermore, the poetry is haunting and, as well as being powerfully evocative of the Duchess' despair, it is also suggestive of the workings of fate, thus making the Duchess' plight seem even more hopeless. Of course, there is a subtle dramatic irony here. As the tale has been told before, and as it is based on historical events, the tragic denouement that she is careering towards is inevitable.

Bosola's role, as usual, is ambiguous and we can never be sure of his genuine feelings and motivation. We should be rightly wary of the **'gold and sugar'** coating of his words, which, as the Duchess suggests, are most likely **'poisoned pills'**; nothing he says can be taken at face value. His praise of the Duchess to Ferdinand is impressive and appears to carry conviction but he is still a very committed master of ceremonies in Ferdinand's appalling treatment of the Duchess. However, his loyalty does appear to have been severely tested and he demands to know Ferdinand's motives, urging him to 'go no further in your cruelty'. He encourages Ferdinand to offer his sister opportunities for penitence. Bosola's refusal to see her again in his own person, and his assertion that if he does return to her 'The business shall be comfort', does seem to suggest a degree of genuine remorse in the part he has so far played in her torture.

Act IV scene 2

The madmen are brought in and present a grotesque **antimasque**. Bosola, disguised, prepares the Duchess to meet her death. The Duchess, the children and Cariola are then all murdered and Bosola shows Ferdinand his sister's body. Ferdinand blames Bosola for carrying out his instructions, denies him any reward except a pardon for the murders, and leaves, distracted. The Duchess revives long enough for Bosola to tell her that Antonio is alive, then she dies. Bosola claims to feel remorse.

Commentary: This scene is the play's dramatic and emotional climax as the conflict between the protagonist and the chief antagonist, Ferdinand, finally comes to a head. Most unusually, this climax occurs here rather than at the end of Act V. (For more on this see the Dramatic arc section of the 'Form, structure and language' chapter, p. 55.) The antics of the madmen can be seen as symbolic of how reason and order have broken down in the world of the play. The death scene in which the Duchess, Cariola and the Duchess' two infant children are strangled is very closely modelled on Painter's account, whereas the preceding episode with the madmen, as well as the twisted psychology exhibited in the remarkable aftermath scene between Bosola and Ferdinand, are of Webster's own devising.

As one would expect in a tragedy, Webster presents his heroine with both compassion and grandeur. At the start of the scene, the Duchess is remarkably self-possessed and calmly analytical of her emotional state. She is very aware of her continued sanity, in contrast to the madmen who Ferdinand has provided in his desperate attempt to make her as deranged as himself.

It is the arch-fiend, Bosola, who is responsible for the management of the Duchess' death, initially appearing in the guise of a tomb-maker. It is difficult to regard the supposed spiritual 'preparation' that he provides for her as anything more than a mocking continuation of her psychological torture. Firstly, he confronts her with an image of physical mortality by referring to her as 'a box of worm-seed'. Then, with seeming relish, he again tries to diminish her high social position by describing her as 'some great woman'.

She responds with resignation and dignity, defiantly asserting her status as 'Duchess of Malfi still' in a triumphant affirmation of her identity in the face of Bosola's concerted attempt to undermine her nobility. When she finally demonstrates her humility by kneeling to enter 'heaven gates', Webster protects the Duchess from the charge of impiety that Painter used to condemn his Duchess as a result of her feigned pilgrimage to Loreto.

Bosola's disguise during these proceedings shows cowardice, his treatment of Cariola is contemptuous and brutal, and his instruction for the killing of the children is shocking in its off-handedness. That his motivation is entirely selfish is indicated by his being so quick to demand his reward and by the way he finds himself 'neglected' – a word he repeats in summing up his role at the end of the play (V.5) – upon being offered no more than a pardon. All of this calls into question the genuineness of the modicum of compassion that he appeared to show for the Duchess in the previous scene. It is also difficult to believe his assertion that he 'loathed the evil' he was required to perform but 'loved' the master who commanded it, since he abandons that master, Ferdinand, the minute he is sure that no reward will be forthcoming. A morality that apparently values being 'a true servant' higher than being 'an honest man' is extremely questionable.

More problematic still is the question of whether the grief and repentance that Bosola displays after Ferdinand's exit are genuine. The soliloquy that ends the scene, it might be argued, reveals for the first time Bosola in the grip of raw emotion. One cannot help but remember, though, that his chief concern appears to be that the Duchess would live so that he might yet have a chance of salvation in 'heaven'. His feelings are still firmly centred on his own personal outcomes rather than on anything to do with the Duchess.

Ferdinand's response to his dead sister, 'Cover her face. Mine eyes dazzle', reveals the depth of his grief. His blaming Bosola for obeying his orders and his abdication of responsibility for the Duchess' murder on the grounds of his mental distraction is both unexpected and breath-taking in its hypocrisy. This inability to face up to

Build critical skills

Do you think less of Webster's skill as a dramatist when you take into account how much of *The Duchess of Malfi* is based on the work of William Painter?

what he has done also heralds the onset of his lycanthropia, his complete break with a reality that he can no longer face: 'I'll go hunt the badger, by owl-light.' With the death of his sister, and the loss of her 'light' from his life, he has — both physically and spiritually — been plunged into a world of darkness.

Act V scene 1

Milan. Antonio, ignorant of his wife's death, discusses with Delio the likelihood of being reconciled to her brothers. Delio is doubtful. In order to discern to whom Antonio's confiscated lands are being given, Delio petitions Pescara. Pescara refuses Delio's request for the lands. He bestows them instead, at the Cardinal's request, to Julia, giving the reason that it would dishonour Delio to take a gift arising from the wrongs done to Antonio. Antonio determines to confront the Cardinal in person.

Commentary: The audience, having just witnessed the Duchess' death, is brought up short by the realisation that nobody knows about it except those who were directly involved, thus imparting a painful **dramatic irony** to Antonio's vain hope of reconciliation with his brothers-in-law. Antonio yet again seems weak here and his determination to confront the Cardinal smacks of both naivety and desperation. This impression is emphasised by his concealment during the dialogue between Delio, Pescara and Julia.

The central incident of the scene, relating to Pescara's granting of the citadel to Julia in preference to Delio, demonstrates the brothers' underhanded dealings in relation to Antonio despite their promises of 'safe conduct'. It also allows Webster to present Pescara as a model of moral uprightness, in contrast to the corruption that operates elsewhere in the play. Pescara does, though, seem impotent in the face of his political masters' wickedness, of which he is evidently well aware, and this is further testament to the theme of morally corrupt leaders unrelentingly creating a morally corrupt society, which Webster set out through Antonio's opening speech right at the start of the play.

This scene also contains important narrative hooks that generate suspense regarding future developments, specifically the nature of Ferdinand's illness and Antonio's projected midnight visit to the Cardinal. The first of these is taken up as soon as the next scene begins.

Dramatic irony: a literary technique, originally used in the theatre of Ancient Greece, which occurs when the audience is privy to information from which characters have been deliberately excluded.

Act V scene 2

Ferdinand is diagnosed with lycanthropia and a doctor unsuccessfully endeavours to treat him. Bosola enters and the Cardinal acts as if he believes the Duchess to be alive, and then engages Bosola to murder Antonio. Julia attempts to seduce Bosola, who in turn decides to use her to find out if the Cardinal's ignorance of the Duchess' death is genuine and to discover the cause of the Cardinal's 'melancholy'. As Bosola secretly observes their conversation, the Cardinal admits that four nights earlier he had ordered that the Duchess and her two infant children be strangled. He then proceeds to murder Julia by making her kiss a poisoned Bible. Bosola agrees to help the Cardinal conceal Julia's murder and to murder Antonio, but in private he resolves to save Antonio.

Commentary: This is a complex scene packed with plot developments, most of them unexpected. There is classic comic relief in the first part, the humour arising from a number of sources: the image of Ferdinand prowling graveyards, digging up corpses, carrying off a dead man's dismembered limb and then howling like a wolf; the physical comedy of Ferdinand's leaping on his shadow and then beating the pompously over-confident doctor; and the withering verbal humour arising from Pescara's sarcastic comment, 'Doctor, he did not fear you throughly'.

This is deftly contrasted with the tragic intensity of the remainder of the scene: the exposure of just how morally corrupt the Cardinal is in having suborned the execution of the Duchess and her family, and the shocking manner in which he blasphemously orchestrates Julia's sudden demise through use of his Bible! Even amid this gravitas, however, Webster cannot resist reintroducing a darkly comic note with Bosola's wryly cynical response to Julia's murder, 'Oh foolish woman, / Couldst not thou have poisoned him?'

Julia's actions – her lust-at-first-sight response to Bosola, her phallic waving of a pistol in his face and her talk of Bosola having arranged for a 'love-powder' to be slipped into her drink – are a perfect parody of the earlier scenes of wooing, concealment and union played out by the Duchess, Antonio and Cariola. The difference is that while the Duchess was modest and blushing, Julia is brash and bold; and while Cariola was a concealed friend to Antonio and the Duchess, Bosola is a concealed enemy to the Cardinal and is merely using Julia to achieve his own ends.

By arousing laughter of various kinds in this scene, Webster underscores the futility of his characters' attempts to fulfil their worldly and generally immoral ambitions. In particular, he greatly diminishes Ferdinand's dramatic stature. There are signs that the Cardinal, too, is losing his grip at this stage of events. It is notable that Webster gives him three moments in this scene where he makes asides to the audience, the first time he has done so in the play, suggesting a need to share his growing anxiety. In other respects, his Machiavellian nature is still confidently at work, whether in inventing an explanation for Ferdinand's mental state, concealing his knowledge of the Duchess' death or, more characteristically, commissioning Bosola to murder Antonio. In doing this, he suggests a variety of subtle ways in which Bosola might discover Antonio's whereabouts. The poisoned Bible with which he murders Julia is a fitting emblem of his evil and hypocrisy.

In confronting the Cardinal, Bosola maintains his persona as the malcontent not yet paid for his 'service', and once again he agrees to carry out grisly crimes for a powerful master, but this time his intentions are only self-seeking in the sense of wishing to appease his conscience through saving Antonio and avenging the Duchess' death, as opposed to his previous characteristic motive – to rise in society at all costs. Webster signifies the authenticity of Bosola's new-found 'morality' by closing the scene with a **sententia** expressed in soliloquy, which employs an image drawn from the words of Christ as spoken in the Garden of

Build critical skills

Why does Webster mix black humour with tragedy?

Taking it further ▶

Search 'Joe Orton plays' on the internet and consider to what extent Orton's work may have been influenced by that of Webster.

Build critical skills

Is there any evidence to suggest that Bosola had hoped to find love with Julia, or is his dismay once again based on thwarted self-interest?

Build critical skills

Why does Webster create so many parallel scenes?

Sententiae: succinct sayings that impart a profound moral or philosophical truth (a feature of Classical drama). In Elizabethan and Jacobean drama, they often appear at the ends of scenes in rhymed couplets.

TASK
Look for other examples of Webster's use of sententiae and consider whether there is a common thread of moral or philosophical insight being developed in this way.

Gethsemane shortly before his arrest and eventual crucifixion: 'O penitence, let me truly taste thy cup, / That throws men down, only to raise them up.'

Context
Webster's use of the cup metaphor deliberately echoes Christ's appeal to God to have the cruel fate of crucifixion lifted from him: 'My Father, if it is possible, may this cup be taken from me' (Luke 22:39).

Julia, previously a shadowy minor character, is unexpectedly elevated in this scene to a central narrative status. When she declares in her death speech, ''Tis weakness / Too much to think what should have been done', she, like the Duchess, remains true to the course she has pursued in life, thus revealing her as a courageous and independent woman to the last breath. She has refused, like the Duchess, to conform to society's expectations of her and has died as she has lived, not reneging in death on her philosophy in life. Her closing words, 'I go I know not whither', are one of Webster's most poignant reminders to his God-fearing audience of a judgement beyond death and, in Julia's case, the question of heaven or hell is uncertain as she has certainly not been 'good', but then neither has she been particularly evil.

CRITICAL VIEW
Whereas the Duchess' death is a historical inevitability, the character of Julia is Webster's own invention and thus a feminist critique might argue that her death reflects the social expectation that such independently minded women must be severely punished.

Act V scene 3
Outside the window of the Cardinal's lodgings in the fort, Delio and Antonio's conversation awakens the local echo, which throws back their words in the form of ominous warnings in what sounds like the Duchess' voice. Delio promises to bring Antonio's son and join him in confronting the Cardinal.

Commentary: This haunting and moving scene gives a sense of Antonio in communion with the spirit of his dead wife, with the painful irony that he believes her to be alive. Antonio's determination to confront the Cardinal is challenged by both Delio and the warnings of the echo, which both offer a gloomy sense of foreboding that generates considerable suspense as they foreshadow Antonio's tragic fate. Antonio comments that the echo is 'very like my wife's voice' and by this device Webster is able to reintroduce the presence of the play's deceased heroine. There is an atmosphere of gothic mystery with the disembodied voice, the midnight setting and the abbey ruins.

Build critical skills
In what way does Delio's counselling of Antonio here 'echo' Cariola's counselling of the Duchess in Act III scene 2?

Taking it further ▶
Look up the term 'gothic novel' online and then consider how far this later tradition may have been influenced by English Renaissance dramas such as *The Duchess of Malfi*.

Act V scene 4

The Cardinal makes Pescara and the other lords promise to stay in their rooms no matter what they may hear, telling them that he may test their promise by making noises of distress himself. In the darkness, Bosola enters the lodgings as planned and overhears the Cardinal determine to kill him when he has served his purpose. Mistaking Antonio for an assassin, Bosola stabs him, realising his error only when the servant returns with the light. He tells Antonio before he dies that his wife and two youngest children are dead, then orders the servant to take Antonio's body to Julia's lodging and determines to kill the Cardinal.

Commentary: In the first part of the scene, Webster once more displays his disconcerting habit of combining black comedy with tragedy. Notable in this respect is the Cardinal's ludicrous suggestion that he might 'feign / Some of [Ferdinand's] mad tricks' in order to test the lords' adherence to their promise. Malateste's assurance that he would not assist the Cardinal were his throat being cut, and that the reason Ferdinand's chamber shook in the storm that night was because of the kindness of the Devil in rocking his own child, help to establish this sense of macabre humour. Equally, this dark humour also serves the more serious purpose of contributing to the impression of evil and of a world in great upheaval.

> **Context**
>
> The Cardinal confiding in the audience that he finds himself unable to pray is reminiscent of the villain Claudius in Shakespeare's *Hamlet* (1603).

> **Context**
>
> Storms are often used for effect in Renaissance drama. Shakespeare makes great use of storm imagery in both *Macbeth* (1606) and *King Lear* (1606), to signify impending social chaos.

The second part of the scene requires careful staging if the 'direful misprision' of Antonio's death is to have a shocking and tragic impact. There should be no possibility that Bosola might recognise Antonio before killing him. There are few stage directions, but Webster makes it plain that it is still night time through the dialogue prior to Antonio being struck down. He also makes it clear that the stage is dark and that Antonio does not have a lantern and, therefore, his features are not readily visible. Bosola's scheming goes as desperately awry as the Cardinal's, suggesting a universe devoid of a controlling moral virtue, in which human beings, as Bosola concludes, are **'merely the stars' tennis balls'**.

> **Top ten quotation**

For those critics who consider Antonio to be a weak, ineffectual character throughout the play, the manner of his death is entirely appropriate, a case of mistaken identity while he is still vainly pursuing reconciliation with his brothers-in-law. We must remember, however, that the option of becoming the determined avenger is denied him as he does not learn until too late about the murder of his wife and children. His tragedy is that of an essentially good man caught up in events that he is not socially eminent enough, or possibly personally strong enough, to control. His dying speech creates considerable sympathy, showing him to be resigned to death since life without the Duchess has no meaning for him.

> **Build critical skills**
>
> Consider why, in a world in which there was such a profound belief in God, there are so many references to fate.

Act V scene 5

CRITICAL VIEW

A feminist critique might suggest that by shaping the resolution of the play as an all-male affair, Webster is once more acknowledging the patriarchal nature of Jacobean society.

Taking it further ▶

For an even more explicit dramatisation of this important theme of the futility of worldly ambition, search online for a synopsis of Christopher Marlowe's *Dr Faustus* (1592), in which a celebrated and highly ambitious academic, descended from 'parents base of stock', sells his soul to Satan for twenty-four years of fame and fortune.

As the Cardinal fearfully contemplates hell, Bosola enters with Antonio's body and announces his intention to kill the Cardinal. The Cardinal's cries for assistance are interpreted by the lords as a test of their promise, but Pescara decides to intervene. Bosola kills the servant to prevent him from admitting help, and then stabs the Cardinal twice. Ferdinand enters and, now totally unhinged, imagines that he is in the battle that he had pined for at the beginning of the play. He wounds the already injured Cardinal and inflicts a 'death wound' on Bosola, who fatally stabs him in return. Ferdinand dies before the lords break in, and the Cardinal dies shortly after. Bosola paints a bleak and hopeless picture of human existence before he too dies. Delio arrives with the Duchess' and Antonio's eldest son and requests the lords' support in establishing the boy as heir to the dukedom.

Commentary: Although 'revenge tragedy' was not identified as a distinct literary genre at the time, the audience would have certain expectations of this type of play and so in this final scene the stage gradually fills up with corpses, thus not only providing spectator satisfaction but simultaneously underlining a moral that might best be summed up by Romans 12:19: 'Vengeance is mine; I will repay, saith the Lord.'

Despite having died at the end of Act IV, Webster keeps the Duchess ever present as other characters acknowledge her central importance. Bosola presents her murder as being of universal significance, in that it creates an unbalancing of 'Justice', resulting in a violent aftermath. For Ferdinand, his sister is the primary factor in a tragic culmination of events: 'My sister! Oh my sister, there's the cause on't!'

Certain key characters in this scene muse on the pointlessness of life, with Ferdinand considering the world to be a 'dog-kennel' and Bosola envisaging it as a 'deep pit of darkness'. This sense of futility also occurs when Bosola explains that Antonio's death came about 'in a mist', reminding us of his earlier reference to life as 'a general mist of error' (IV.2). But perhaps Webster means these statements to be reflections on these characters' own misspent paths rather than on human existence in general. As the Cardinal philosophically declares, 'Sorrow is held the eldest child of sin'.

CRITICAL VIEW

L.G. Salingar perceives a socio-political dimension to such dramatic denouements: 'the middle-class desire for the rule of law and fear of a recrudescence of feudalism are leading motives … in the series of revenge tragedies, from Kyd onwards' ('The Social Setting' in *The Pelican Guide to English Literature, Volume 2*, 1963). Thus Webster's emphasis upon personal merit can be viewed as a direct challenge to the traditional prerogative which granted great social prestige and power to a narrow elite whose only claim to such advantage was the good fortune of having been high-born. Salingar's approach here certainly supports a Marxist critical perspective.

Once all the death speeches have been concluded, Delio promotes Antonio's eldest son as heir to the dukedom of Malfi, conveniently neglecting the rightful inheritor, the Duchess' son by her first husband (referred to earlier by Ferdinand at the end of Act III scene 3). Webster may well be signalling Delio's awareness of this other, more legitimate claim by his declaration that it will need 'all our force' to establish Antonio's son to power. To add a final frisson to this question of the boy's succession, we might recall the horoscope from Act II scene 3, which predicted for the boy a 'short life' and 'a violent death'. Thus the cycle of ambition, rivalry and revenge may be set to continue.

Webster closes with yet another echo of earlier events. Delio, the character who opened the play, now ends it by succinctly summarising the deeply Christian subtext of this great drama, which is that worldly success is ephemeral and therefore ultimately worthless. Not only has Webster already dramatically illustrated this with the violent deaths of Ferdinand and the Cardinal, but he also has Ferdinand remind the audience, just prior to his own expiration, of the violent demises of two of the greatest Ancient Romans, Pompey and Caesar, who were both betrayed and ultimately ignobly stabbed to death.

Context

One could infer the entire meaning of *The Duchess of Malfi* from the question posed by Jesus: 'For what is a man profited, if he shall gain the whole world, and lose his own soul?' (Matthew 16:26).

TASK

Read the synopsis of William Painter's *Duchess of Malfy* (see the Appendix on p. 93 of this guide) or follow the weblink to the full text (see Taking it Further on p. 97). Painter's version of Bandello's original account of the historical Duchess of Amalfi overwhelmingly provides Webster with his main source material for the play. Make a note of the similarities and differences between the two. Then, list some of Webster's possible reasons for deviating in the ways he does from Painter's account.

Target your thinking

- What are the key themes and how does Webster develop them as the dramatic action unfolds? (**AO1**)
- What dramatic methods does Webster use to illustrate his key themes? (**AO2**)

When we write about Webster's handling of a particular theme, we should remember that he was not writing an academic treatise but a drama, which was primarily constructed to entertain and which had the further **didactic** purpose of providing moral instruction. Therefore, his themes are essentially the big ideas of topical interest at that time, which he explores as he strives to entertain and instruct.

The hollowness of worldly status

When the Duchess declares 'I am Duchess of Malfi still', Bosola responds with the sententia that 'Glories, like glow worms, afar off shine bright, / But looked to near, have neither heat nor light' (IV.2). Sententiae are succinct sayings that impart a profound moral or philosophical truth. Although Bosola is almost certainly being his characteristically antagonistic and contrary self, one of the play's central themes is undoubtedly the deceptive attractiveness of worldly status. Fame, glory, power and ambition are all demonstrated in the play as failing to offer either happiness or lasting moral value. Therefore, the play becomes a form of ethical quest for a way of living that offers deeper emotional satisfaction and moral integrity. The Duchess finds such a life with Antonio but it is destroyed by the morally corrupt individuals in control of this society.

Webster has Delio crystallise this message in the closing speech of the play, with his summation of Ferdinand and the Cardinal: 'These wretched eminent things / Leave no more fame behind 'em than should one / Fall in a frost and leave his print in snow…' The metaphor clearly reflects the Bible's emphasis on the transitory nature of life. As Webster has Delio conclude, again in sententia, what really matters is how a life has been conducted: 'Integrity of life is fame's best friend, / Which nobly, beyond death, shall crown the end.' The reference to a judgement beyond the grave is explicit.

The nature of nobility

In Jacobean society, the word 'noble' could refer to inherent moral worth, but it could also be used to refer to a person of extremely high birth. Webster provides

Build critical skills

Consider whether a sententia retains any moral force if it is delivered by an immoral character such as Bosola.

CRITICAL VIEW

In his 1610 speech to Parliament, King James declared that 'Kings are justly called gods'. A Marxist critique might suggest that by having the two main powerbrokers murdered by a mere servant, Webster is attempting to demythologise state power.

a salutary reminder in Act II that, regardless of rank, all men share a common humanity. Given the rigidly hierarchical nature of Jacobean society, this was a revolutionary theme. Bosola declares to Antonio:

> Some would think the souls of princes were brought forth by some more weighty cause than those of meaner persons; they are deceived, there's the same hand to them, the like passions sway them; the same reason that makes a vicar go to law for a tithe-pig, and undo his neighbours, makes them spoil a whole province, and batter down goodly cities with the cannon.

(II.1)

In Act II scene 3, Webster uses Antonio's sententia to make a similar point: **'The great are like the base, nay, they are the same, / When they seek shameful ways to avoid shame.'** Both the rich and the poor are guided by similar passions and the only real difference between them is their social position, not any innate quality that makes one better or lesser than the other. As the action of the play makes clear, the two most powerful figures in the play, Ferdinand and the Cardinal, are mean-spirited individuals driven by base and ignoble desires.

CRITICAL VIEW

A Marxist perspective may well politicise the point by adding that the only real difference between a socially eminent person and a person of a meaner status, is that the powerful have more power to do harm.

Top ten quotation

Meritocracy

Equally as radical is Bosola's argument in favour of a **meritocracy** in Act III scene 2, when applauding the Duchess on preferring 'A man merely for worth'. Some critics will quickly explain this away as part of his cynical attempt to deceive the Duchess and win her confidence so that he can then betray her to her brothers – which, of course, is exactly what he does. But once again, this allows Webster to distance himself from a very dangerous social concept while still being able eloquently to commend the idea. And, of course, although we should be sceptical of Bosola's motives here, the idea that he expresses perfectly befits his character and thus is most likely honestly felt. Furthermore, it is also an idea that the audience is being implicitly encouraged to applaud because it eloquently crystallises exactly what the play's heroine, the radiant and enchanting Duchess, has done when following her heart and marrying the virtuous Antonio. As always, however, Bosola remains enigmatic. The Duchess' dog-fish parable in Act III scene 5, in which she also seems to support a meritocracy, is actually in response to Bosola's apparent sudden reversal of attitude when he describes Antonio as 'this base, low fellow' and as 'One of no birth'.

Meritocracy: a fluid society in which people are promoted on the basis of talent and achievement.

Build critical skills

How far does Bosola really mean what he says when he attacks Antonio's comparatively lowly origin in Act III scene 5?

Puritanical age: this was a society in which a fundamentalist belief in the Bible strictly censored how people should behave.

Context

Ambition was one of the chief moral concerns of this puritanical age because it often led to ruthless self-interest: ''Tis not law / Nor conscience that can keep this fiend in awe' (George Withers, *Of Ambition*, 1613).

Context

Using a conversational format in which fictional characters exchange opposing points of view was a common device at this time for presenting radical and potentially dangerous ideas, e.g. Galileo's *Dialogue Concerning the Two Chief World Systems* (1632). Thinly disguised as a philosophical discussion between three friends, Galileo was really arguing for the supremacy of the Copernican model of the solar system in which all the planets (including the Earth) revolved around the sun. By presenting his conclusions in this way, Galileo (unsuccessfully) hoped to escape the wrath of the Catholic Church which steadfastly maintained that the Earth was at the centre of everything. (See the *New philosophy* section on p.32 of this guide.)

Ambition

Despite all the indications that Webster may have favoured a meritocracy ('this ambitious age' as he has Bosola term it in Act III scene 2), there is, as is often the case with this play, a problematic ambiguity. Having very possibly trained as a lawyer, Webster may have done this intentionally, as it would allow him wiggle-room should he fall foul of the state censor. Consequently, ambition is also portrayed as something that is dangerous to both self and society:

Antonio: 'Ambition, Madam, is a great man's madness…'

(I.1)

Delio: 'I do fear / Antonio is betrayed. How fearfully / Shows his ambition now…'

(II.4)

Ferdinand: 'Whether we fall by ambition, blood, or lust, / Like diamonds we are cut with our own dust.'

(V.5)

Build critical skills

On balance, to what extent do you think Webster is in favour of social mobility?

Social inequality

The social mismatch between the Duchess and Antonio is referred to on a number of occasions throughout the play. Initially, the theme is introduced by the Duchess' delicate courting of Antonio towards the end of Act I, when she laments: 'The misery of us that are born great, / We are forced to woo because none dare woo us…' (I.1). Being a spiritual person herself, she is attracted by Antonio's virtue and not by his social status: **'This goodly roof of yours is too low built'** (I.1). Most other characters who comment on the match after their relationship becomes public, however, merely reflect the prejudices of

Top ten quotation

the time. The compassionate First Pilgrim remarks, 'Here's a strange turn of state: who would have thought / So great a lady would have matched herself / Unto so mean a person?' (III.4). And as we have just seen, Bosola – although he continually rails against a system that denies him the status he believes he deserves – will also use the prejudice if it suits him.

Corruption and sycophancy

Through the prism of the Italian court settings and one hundred years of history, Webster is able to allude to the well-known misconduct in King James' Court. Webster presents a world of sycophants desperate to advance their own position, regardless of the consequences to others. Again, it is Bosola's pithy prose that crystallises the theme: 'places in the court are but like beds in the hospital, where this man's head lies at that man's foot, and so lower, and lower' (I.1). The simile conjures up an impression of a sick society in which courtiers eagerly await the opportunity to benefit from the deaths or misfortunes of those above them. Thus Bosola's dark comparison extends the vision initially set out by Antonio's sententia in the play's opening: **'but if 't chance / Some cursed example poison 't near the head, / Death and diseases through the whole land spread'** (I.1). (For much more on this central theme, see the King James' court section of the 'Contexts' chapter, p. 65.)

> **Context**
>
> In 1610, Robert Carr persuaded King James to dissolve Parliament because of its desire to regulate the royal finances, something that would have personally affected Carr's ability to continue to acquire wealth from James.

Flattery

Inextricably interwoven with the above is the equally important theme of flattery, a well-known strategy employed by King James' favourites in order to advance their position in court – despite their frequent lack of ability or good character. In Act III scene 1, Webster makes clear the damage that their insincerity causes as they fluff up the egos of the powerful in their dedication to parasitic self-interest, thus encouraging rulers to lose all sense of reality. Bosola's refusal (or inability!) to flatter Ferdinand brings forth the following response from the Duke: 'I never gave pension but to flatterers / Till I entertained thee: farewell. / That friend a great man's ruin strongly checks, / Who rails into his belief, all his defects.'

Antonio, on the other hand, always puts a disinterested moral perspective on flattery while still warning of exactly the same dangers. In his opening speech in the play, he refers to the political and moral necessity that a 'judicious king / … quits first his royal palace / Of flatt'ring sycophants, of dissolute / And infamous persons…' What Webster appears to be advocating is a king safe-guarded

> **Build critical skills**
>
> What dramatic devices does Webster employ to enable him to get away with his portrayal of the corruption of James' system of government before an audience that included educated aristocracy?

Top ten quotation

> **Context**
>
> Victorian Prime Minister Benjamin Disraeli once said, 'Everyone likes flattery; and when you come to Royalty you should lay it on with a trowel.'

Top ten quotation

from duplicitous flatterers by wise advisors: 'And what is 't makes this blessed government / But a most provident council, who dare freely / Inform him the corruption of the times?' (I.1).

(See the King James' court section of the 'Contexts' chapter, p. 65.)

A new social order?

There are many references to 'the devil' and to 'hell' in the play because the society that Webster's characters inhabit has two 'cursed examples' at its head. But Antonio's vision describes a 'blessed government'. It might be argued, therefore, that Webster was hinting that it was time the social order was replaced with something more in line with the laws of nature, where people would not be judged on the circumstance of their birth, nor promoted through their willingness to pander to the socially privileged, but rather would be judged on moral worth and rewarded on the basis of merit through fair and open means – in other words, a meritocracy (see p. 25).

Webster seems to be suggesting that a society where a person's birth grants or denies them privilege is against the laws of nature, as is emphasised when the Duchess states that **'The birds that live i'th'field / On the wild benefit of nature, live / Happier than we; for they may choose their mates…'** (III.5). In marrying Antonio, she has extended the power base – so jealously guarded by the likes of the Cardinal and Ferdinand – to include the low-born. In simple terms, the larger the ruling class, the fewer the riches for each member of that class. This is why the Duchess' actions are utterly unacceptable. Webster, though, seems to see positives in her subversion of the social balance. If so, then he has radically departed from the sentiment expressed in his source material, Painter's *The Palace of Pleasure*: 'Shall I be of opinion that a houshold seruaunt oughte to sollicite, nay rather suborne the Daughter of his Lorde without punyshment, or that a vyle and abiect person dare to mount vpon a Prynces Bed? No, no, pollicye requyreth order in all, and eche wight ought to bee matched according to theyr qualytye…'.

We see this again when Bosola enthusiastically asks 'Can this ambitious age / Have so much goodness in 't as to prefer / A man merely for worth, without these shadows / Of wealth and painted honours?' (III.2). Of course, Bosola's intention at this point in the play is to deceive the Duchess and win over her confidence so that he can betray her to her brothers. Equally, though, his glowing declaration could be interpreted, as the Duchess sees it, as a tribute to her courage and moral foresightedness for being willing to defy such a powerful social convention, by which a ruthless political elite selfishly clings on to the power and wealth that they have inherited merely through birthright.

Delio's final words, however, appear to suggest that if change is going to occur it will still have to come from the top, and it will not happen without a struggle against the vested interest. It will take the willingness of all the virtuous members of the nobility to **'join all our force / To establish this young hopeful gentleman / In's mother's right'** (V.5). But as with so much in the world of the play, even the 'final' resolution is deeply ambiguous. There is a 'new order' to the extent that the new prince is descended from a virtuous father who is a commoner. Furthermore, it would appear that this prince will be able to benefit from the council of such wise and virtuous men as Delio and Pescara. It is difficult, however, to forget either the horoscope discovered by Bosola in Act II that augured 'a violent death' (II.3) for the young prince, or the fact that the Duchess' eldest child by her first husband, who is a prince of truly noble blood, is out there somewhere, lurking in the wings.

In the opening scene, Antonio tells Delio: 'Though some o'th'court hold it presumption / To instruct princes what they ought to do, / It is a noble duty to inform them / What they ought to foresee' (I.1). Perhaps the play was Webster's own way of fulfilling this 'noble duty'.

Top ten quotation

Women's roles

In *The Duchess of Malfi*, Webster places the restrictions and pressures imposed upon women under sympathetic scrutiny. The frequent misogynistic remarks uttered by a number of the male characters – such as the conversations of Ferdinand and the Duchess in Act I, Bosola with the Old Lady in Act II scene 1, and the Cardinal with Julia in Act II scene 4 – are not countered explicitly but are proved false through the integrity and courage of the Duchess.

The Duchess' marriage to Antonio elicits popular disapproval by flouting social convention in a number of ways: she has married in secret without the blessing of the Church; secondly, she has married in defiance of her brothers' express wishes; thirdly, her husband is of a much-inferior social status. These circumstances would have been seen as dangerously subversive to both social stability and religious orthodoxy. Webster, however, offers a sympathetic view of the marriage by stressing the corruption of the Duchess' brothers and presenting touching scenes of wooing and domesticity.

The unconventional Julia is the opposite of the Duchess, being both 'wanton' and 'lustful'. She is quite unabashed, dismissing 'modesty' as 'but a troublesome familiar' (V.2) that holds women back from fulfilling their natural desires. Many modern audiences would relish Julia's character and find much to admire in her outright rejection of the moral constraints imposed upon her sex by men. In her death, too, she neither seeks solace in ideas of heaven nor fearfully predicts hell as her destination, but philosophically maintains that it is 'weakness' to moralise about the life we have led at the last, and states that she goes 'I know not whither' (V.2).

Love and lust

The play explores the varieties of physical and emotional attraction that motivate human relationships. On the darker side, there is Ferdinand's suppressed desire for his sister and the Cardinal's lust for Julia. Julia herself

CRITICAL VIEW

A Marxist perspective might find Webster's proposals no more than a minor adjustment of the status quo, especially in light of the truly radical social ideas of the **Levellers** that arose during the English Civil Wars (1642–51).

Levellers: a political movement during the English Civil War that emphasised popular sovereignty, extended rights to vote, legal equality and religious tolerance.

Build critical skills

In light of this play, in what ways do you think Webster could be considered as a proto-feminist?

CRITICAL VIEW

A feminist perspective might point out that Julia's behaviour, though not moral, is liberated because she demands the same sexual freedom as men.

is presented partly as a stereotype of subversive female sexuality and is associated with four different men during the course of the play. Her sexual appetites are evidently left unsatisfied by her old and impotent husband; she is shown rejecting the renewed advances of her former suiter, Delio; her relationship with the Cardinal is seen to be at a crucial turning-point as he seems to be tiring of her; and she expresses an instantaneous sexual attraction for Bosola that results in her death.

In contrast, Webster presents the Duchess' love for Antonio and their secret marriage in a sympathetic light, creating a series of scenes between them that are touching and, sometimes, gently amusing. Passionate sexuality is not absent from their relationship, first suggested symbolically in the placing of the ring on his finger and then made explicit in her pregnancy and the apparently rapid growth of their family, and in their bedroom banter at the start of Act III scene 2. Their indulgence in sexual activity is entirely normal and natural, especially when contrasted with Ferdinand's lurid sexual fantasising about their activities in Act II scene 5. The tragedy arises out of the fact that Jacobean society can interpret the Duchess only through the stereotype of the 'lusty widow' (I.1), ultimately condemning her as 'a strumpet' (III.1). This is a designation Webster vehemently contradicts in his overall presentation of her. In fact, Webster's extremely sensitive presentation of the love between Antonio and the Duchess throughout the play provides a dignity to human nature that contrasts powerfully with the frequent animal behaviour of most of the other characters.

Religion

In the world of the play, the Roman Catholic Church is corrupt at its very heart and is motivated by greed for material gain (and England at the time was a Protestant country, full of anti-Catholic fervour). This is illustrated amply in the way the Cardinal has bribed his way up the ecclesiastical hierarchy, redistributes Antonio's lands, has illicit affairs with married women and suborns murder. He is a ruthless politician content to exchange his pastoral responsibilities for military ones. Although the presentation of the Cardinal clearly panders to the anti-Catholic prejudice of its time, Webster may well have been commenting on the worldliness of some of those in powerful positions within the Anglican Church in his own society. For instance, in order to enable King James' favourite, Robert Carr, to marry Frances Howard, it had to be established whether it was possible to nullify her existing marriage to Robert Devereaux. King James packed the commission responsible for deciding this with bishops who would support the annulment. These bishops were primarily guided by the desire of the king to please his favourite rather than by any finer points of conscience. (See of the King James' court section of the 'Contexts' chapter, p. 65.)

Webster's handling of the theme of religion also offers a contrast between true spirituality and the ruthless pursuit of worldly status. It is most appropriate that the Cardinal's first explicitly theological reflections coincide with his imminent downfall, finding him 'puzzled in a question about hell' (V.5), by which Webster has him presumably anticipating his own destiny. The writing is most vivid and expresses genuine terror as it evokes the image of men burning in 'one material fire' and describes the Cardinal's visions of a demon 'armed with a rake / That seems to strike at me.' Bosola is also subject to 'a perspective / That shows us hell' (IV.2) and, similarly, Ferdinand has every expectation of being damned: 'When I go to hell, I mean to carry a bribe...' (V.2).

The Duchess, on the other hand, is virtuous. She is clearly very human, and thus imperfect, but her moral transgressions are minor (see 'Characters', p. 36). When faced with death, she transcends all of these inconsequential defects as a result of her great courage and Christian humility: 'Yet stay, heaven gates are not so highly arched / As princes' palaces: they that enter there / Must go upon their knees' (IV.2).

As stated in the Bible, 'the wages of sin is death' (Romans 6:23). Through the examples of Ferdinand, the Cardinal and Bosola, Webster emulates the fashion of other English Renaissance dramatists and leaves his audience in no doubt that sin leads to both physical and spiritual death.

Fate and destiny

The drama of the English Renaissance also places great emphasis on the influence of the stars and other celestial bodies as determining factors in shaping human affairs. In *The History of the World* (1614), Sir Walter Raleigh addresses 'the dispute and contention concerning fate and destiny' and advises that the 'beautiful stars' are 'instruments and organs of his divine providence...' In so doing, he reflects the spirit of both Classical and Renaissance literature. Raleigh adds the qualification that although 'the stars and other celestial bodies incline the will by mediation of the sensitive appetite', free will is still the crucial factor: 'there is no inclination or temptation so forcible, which our humble prayers and desires may not make frustrate and break asunder...' Thus he rejects Calvinist notions of predestination. In *The Duchess of Malfi*, however, fate seems more predominant than free will, as is exemplified by Bosola's inability to control his own future. Bosola predicates his salvation on ensuring Antonio's survival. As such, the best he can manage when trying to account for the 'direful misprision' of his accidental murdering of Antonio is to lament, 'In a mist: I know not how...' (V.5). In William Painter's version of the story, Bosola murders Antonio with impunity. Webster, therefore, appears to be evoking divine providence in order to damn the unworthy.

Context

A major theological debate of the time within Protestantism was whether a man's eternal destiny in either heaven or hell had already been predestined by God, as advocated by French theologian John Calvin (1509-64), or whether an individual could attain salvation through choosing to lead a morally correct life, a view advocated by the Dutch theologian James Arminius (1560-1609).

Heliocentric: the astronomical model in which the earth and planets revolve around the sun at the centre of the Solar System.

Context

In the opening scene of 'Tis Pity She's a Whore (1633), the Friar warns Giovanni against 'striving how to prove / There was no God ...'

CRITICAL VIEW

'The crisis of the early seventeenth century was a far-reaching conflict of values – between the religious traditions of the Middle Ages and the secular bias of the Renaissance...' (L.G. Salingar, 'The Elizabethan Literary Renaissance' in *The Pelican Guide to English Literature, Volume 2*, 1963).

Zeitgeist: the spirit of the time.

New philosophy

The age-old view that positioned the Earth at the centre of the universe had been challenged by the Copernican revolution, which since 1543 had relegated the Earth to a mere satellite of the sun. Italian scientist Galileo greatly enhanced the status of Copernicus' **heliocentric** universe through use of the telescope, an early seventeenth century invention which Galileo transformed into a much more powerful instrument by greatly increasing its magnification. Galileo's astronomical observations from 1609 onwards revealed hitherto unknown information about the solar system, such as his detection in January 1610 of four moons orbiting Jupiter, a discovery which he then published in Sidereus Nuncius ('The Starry Messenger') in March 1610. This helped to support the idea that the Earth was not the centre of everything as had come to be generally accepted since first propounded by Ptolemy around AD 150. These new discoveries made the biblical account of creation in Genesis seem rather simplistic and ill-informed by comparison.

In 1610, the English ambassador in Venice wrote home: 'I send herewith unto His Majesty the strangest piece of news ... that he has ever yet received from any part of the world ... the Mathematical Professor at Padua ... hath discovered four new planets rolling around the sphere of Jupiter, besides many other unknown fixed stars; likewise the true cause of the Via Lactea [the Milky Way], so long searched; and lastly that the moon is not spherical but endued with many prominences ... he hath overthrown all former astronomy...'

To many, especially within the Catholic Church, Galileo's findings were heresy because by contesting the long-standing Christian cosmology which firmly placed the Earth in the centre of all things they challenged the authority of the Catholic Church itself. Such views could thus undermine fundamental beliefs, including that of Providential Justice, which regarded God's influence as an active force for order within the world. Poet John Donne was acutely sensitive to the destabilising moral, theological and philosophical impact of the emerging empiricism when he lamented: 'And new philosophy calls all in doubt' ('An Anatomy of the World', 1611). The Renaissance quest for knowledge was beginning to unsettle the traditional picture of the universe and thus the medieval world view was falling into crisis.

In *Faultlines: Cultural Materialism and the Politics of Dissident Reading* (1992), Alan Sinfield sees the emerging **zeitgeist** being reflected in Webster's work when he argues that 'in *The Duchess of Malfi*, providential care is far more difficult to discern'. He cites Bosola's accidental killing of Antonio as particularly pertinent in this respect. David Gunby, on the other hand, is equally as convinced that Webster's perception of reality is firmly rooted in traditional Christian certainty, and so perceives 'a complex, moving, and deeply religious vision of human existence' (*John Webster: Three Plays*, 1972).

'Artistic insincerity – a lie in the poet's heart'

One of the most savage attacks upon Webster occurs in *The Case of John Webster* (1949), in which Ian Jack accuses Webster of 'philosophical poverty', declares that he has 'no profound hold on any system of moral values' and adds that 'his attempt to shore up chaos with a sententious philosophy is a flagrant artistic insincerity'. Jack's disdain is based on his perception of a fundamental disconnect between Webster's frequent moral maxims and sententiae, which Jack denounces as 'dissembling verse' borrowed from the tradition of Classical Stoicism, and the worldview that Webster projects in his drama. This 'lie in the poet's heart' (a reference to Webster's play *The White Devil*) is merely a series of rhetorical gestures, which have been bolted on just to appease the puritanical and aesthetic temper of the age. According to Jack, 'In Webster there is no deeper purpose than to make our flesh creep.' He concludes: 'Comfortable words spoken at the end of *The White Devil* and *The Dutchesse of Malfy* carry no conviction; if we take evil away from Webster's world, nothing is left.'

To a large extent, Jack is echoing Henry Peacham's lament in *The Compleat Gentleman* (1622), when he complained of 'Scenical pomp, with empty furniture of phrase, wherewith the Stage, and our petty Poetic Pamphlets sound so big … yet it yieldeth nothing.' But if there is any truth in Jack's critique then, as Peacham indicates, Webster is far from alone in this respect and thus is it seems grossly unfair to single him out for especial calumny.

The ephemeral nature of man

Assuming that there is an explicitly theological and moral intent to *The Duchess of Malfi*, then an equally important and complementary theme is that of the corporeal composition of man. Bosola graphically articulates this shortly before he orders the Duchess' death: 'our bodies are weaker than those paper prisons boys use to keep flies in – more contemptible, since ours is to preserve earth worms' (IV.2).

In the final scene of the play, we are reminded by the deaths of Ferdinand and the Cardinal, and by Ferdinand's reference to Caesar and Pompey, that even great worldly power and status ultimately signifies nothing, and all that really counts is how one's life will be judged after death. Again, it is important to understand the significance of the sententia with which Webster has Delio close the play: 'Integrity of life is fame's best friend, / Which nobly, beyond death, shall crown the end.'

> **TASK**
>
> Compare the ephemeral nature of man in *The Duchess of Malfi* to the transient nature of worldy power presented in Percy Shelley's 'Ozymandias'.

Revenge

The classification of this type of play as being in the 'revenge tragedy' genre is a relatively modern phenomenon, the phrase having been coined by the American literary critic A.H. Thorndike in 1902. The 'revenge tragedy' genre of English

TASK

Make your own list of the ways in which Webster's play conforms to the 'revenge tragedy' genre.

Context

'...So shall you hear / Of carnal, bloody, and unnatural acts, / Of accidental judgements, casual slaughters, / Of deaths put on by cunning and forced cause / And... purposes mistook / Fall'n on the inventors' heads' (William Shakespeare, *Hamlet*, 1603).

literature generally refers to a type of drama written between the mid-1580s and the early 1640s. Typical of these works are the following features:

- the murder of an innocent or good character
- a wronged avenger
- moral and spiritual chaos resulting from a morally decadent society
- a machiavel
- a malcontent
- political intrigue
- the use of disguise and a conflict between appearance and reality
- ghosts
- misogyny
- mental instability and deviant desires
- gratuitous presentations of extreme torture and/or violence, often with considerable realism
- a corpse-strewn conclusion.

Revenge tragedy captures the tension between the medieval tradition of settling personal grievances through violence, such as duelling and blood feuds, and the evolving importance of the legal system in contemporary Renaissance society. In 1614, King James issued 'A proclamation against private challenges and combats' owing to the rising number of such incidents among the upper classes. Revenge tragedies generally have a central avenger whose motivation is established early in the play, e.g. Vindice in *The Revenger's Tragedy*. In *The Duchess of Malfi*, though, while revenge is clearly an important theme, the situation is not so clear-cut. Ferdinand and the Cardinal revenge themselves on their sister for disobeying them, but their destruction of her is out of all proportion to her 'sin'. Bosola then becomes the central revenger, he claims on behalf of Antonio, but Antonio is not even aware that his wife has been killed. Bosola makes the revenge motivation explicit in his explanation of the concluding bloodbath:

'Revenge for the Duchess of Malfi, murdered
By th'Aragonian brethren; for Antonio,
Slain by this hand; for lustful Julia,
Poisoned by this man; and lastly, for myself,
That was an actor in the main of all,
Much 'gainst mine own good nature, yet i' th' end
Neglected.'

(V.5)

This speech contains various layers of irony, one of the most striking being that it was he who was directly responsible for the horrific murder of the Duchess and two of her children and for the accidental killing of Antonio. Furthermore, he inadvertently accelerated the Cardinal's murder of Julia. He clouds the issue, too, by citing himself as a victim rather than the perpetrator that he truly is. Perhaps the true essence of the presentation of revenge within the play, however, is more in the tradition of the morality play. Webster clearly presents the pursuit of vengeance as ultimately self-destructive – for, as the Bible states, revenge is the sole preserve of God: 'Vengeance is mine; I will repay, saith the Lord' (Romans 12:19).

Context

A morality play is a type of drama that was popular in the fifteenth and early sixteenth centuries. It personified abstract qualities, such as revenge, as main characters and thus sought to teach lessons about good conduct. Webster's play is part of a much more sophisticated tradition of drama, in which it is the overall treatment of the theme that conveys its message.

Appearance and reality

For this theme, see Extended commentary 1 on page 87 of this guide and Top Ten quotations 3, 6 and 8 on pages 91–2 of this guide.

Target your thinking

- How does Webster develop his characters as the dramatic action unfolds? (**AO1**)
- What dramatic methods does Webster use to shape the audience's responses to the characters? (**AO2**)

Build critical skills

According to the poet Rupert Brooke (1887–1915), 'The world called Webster' is inhabited by characters who 'kill, love, torture one another blindly and without ceasing.' How far do you agree with this view?

Build critical skills

Is the convention of characters revealing their true selves in soliloquy in any way undermined if other characters are on stage at the same time?

One of the most common errors made by students is to write about characters in literature as if they are real people, when actually they are constructs created to fulfil a range of functions. Examiners will be looking for your understanding of the techniques a writer uses to create particular characters for particular purposes.

Characters in a play are defined through language and action. What they do, what they say, how they say it, and what other characters say about them determines the response of a reader. On stage, these techniques of characterisation are enhanced by costume, gesture, facial expression and other performance features. In examining the text, you need to be sensitive to the characters' use of verse or prose, the rhetorical and figurative qualities of their speech, the imagery (both that which they use and that which is associated with them), and the tone of their language. Characters given soliloquies are placed in a privileged position in relation to members of the audience, who are allowed to share their innermost thoughts.

The Duchess

Webster draws primarily upon William Painter's *The Palace of Pleasure* for his characterisation of the Duchess, although Webster's Duchess is a more dominant partner in the marriage, just as his Antonio is less decisive. As in Painter's version of the story, the heroine is never given a personal name. She is thus automatically invested with a sense of majesty as a result of the consequent emphasis upon her title as 'the Duchess' and by the fact that Webster has her refer to herself as a 'prince' on a number of occasions.

TASK

Read the synopsis of William Painter's *The Palace of Pleasure* on page 93 and make a list of the similarities and differences between Painter's character of the Duchess and Webster's.

Context

Painter, Webster's main source, condemns the Duchess for her marriage to Antonio as, indeed, does Thomas Beard. Beard, a very minor source, denies the legality of her marriage, describing it as 'nothing but plain whoredom and fornication...' (*The Theatre of God's Judgements*, 1597).

Through Antonio's initial eulogy of her to Delio in Act I Webster sets up an idealised portrait of the Duchess by which the audience must judge her throughout the rest of the play. Antonio is clearly infatuated and his description is couched in so many religious references that it makes her sound like a saint. As we soon discover, though, she is fundamentally human, as she herself declares when wooing Antonio towards the end of Act I: 'This is flesh and blood, sir, / 'Tis not the figure cut in alabaster / Kneels at my husband's tomb' (I.1).

As Webster is writing tragedy, however, and the Duchess is clearly the tragic heroine, then according to Aristotle's famous definition of a tragic hero in his *Poetics* (350BCE) (see the Aristotelian Tragedy section of the 'Form, structure and language' chapter on p. 54), she needs to be not just recognisably human but to embody 'some error of judgement or frailty'. The Duchess' 'frailty' is that she has a young woman's desire for love and sexual fulfilment within marriage and her 'error of judgement' is that she pursues this regardless of consequence. In Jacobean society, her defiance of her brothers' authority in order to fulfil this perfectly natural need would have been controversial, as would her readiness and skill in deceit and prevarication. In such a patriarchal society, the punishment for defiance like this could well be death. Furthermore, as Webster was working from real events as related to him via Painter, the Duchess' death is inevitable regardless of any social expectations to which Webster might be responding.

Some critics find fault with the Duchess' individualism, i.e. her abdication of responsibility for affairs of state in favour of domestic bliss, and regard her secretive behaviour, which results in rumour, speculation and innuendo, as negligent because it undermines her authority. Thus it could be argued that it is the Duchess' recklessness in rejecting the social norms of the age that leads to the ultimate destabilisation of her society. Webster seems to recognise the Duchess' choice of love over duty as a frailty when, in the closing lines of Act I, he has Cariola remark, 'Whether the spirit of greatness or of woman / Reign most in her, I know not, but it shows / A fearful madness. I owe her much of pity.'

Regarding the question of her ability as a ruler, a more serious charge that could be laid against her is her frequent lack of political acumen, such as her belief that her brothers can ultimately be reconciled to her secret marriage to Antonio and her extreme naivety in trusting Bosola in Act III scene 2, a mistake that ultimately leads to the horrific murders of her and her two youngest children. In dramatic terms, however, her gullibility here is an electrifying moment and perhaps Webster is more concerned with plot development at this point than with characterisation.

TASK

Re-read the Duchess' death speech in Act IV scene 2. She may not have lived like a saint, but to what extent do you think she dies like one?

Taking it further ▶

Using an online synopsis of Shakespeare's *Romeo and Juliet*, consider the similarities between these two tragic heroines.

CRITICAL VIEW

'…unconcerned with her duchy's political health, the Duchess seeks private happiness at the expense of public stability. As a ruler, she can no more be lauded for the example that she sets than her brothers.' (Lee Bliss, *The World's Perspective: John Webster and the Jacobean Drama*, 1983).

CRITICAL VIEW

In *Poetics*, Aristotle states: 'The plot, then, is the first principle, and, as it were, the soul of a tragedy; Character holds the second place.'

CRITICAL VIEW

A feminist perspective would most likely reject any criticism of the Duchess' responsibility for the social meltdown that occurs, viewing this more as a condemnation of male-dominated Jacobean society itself.

Webster further humanises the Duchess, thus rounding out her character and ultimately making her even more sympathetic, through her chastisement of her servants, which was a frequent social norm of the age. In Act II scene 1, she petulantly upbraids the Old Lady for having bad breath when Bosola makes a seemingly casual remark that calls attention to the fact that the Duchess might be secretly pregnant. In Act III scene 2 she calls the faithful Cariola 'a superstitious fool' for cautioning against Bosola's questionable advice that the Duchess should 'feign a pilgrimage' in order to make good her escape from her brothers. In her defence, though, such behaviour is infrequent and both are intensely stressful situations where her life is at stake. Furthermore, elsewhere in the play she is presented as being playful and affectionate in domestic situations with both Antonio and Cariola, and she is a loving and caring mother.

Context

In 1574, Queen Elizabeth I is reported to have flown into such a rage when Mary Scudamore, one of her gentlewomen, secretly married without her consent that she actually broke Mary's finger. The Duchess' transgressions are of a significantly lesser order.

CRITICAL VIEW

'The characterisation of the Duchess … is one calculated to inspire pity to a degree very rare indeed in any tragical poetry' (Edmund Gosse, *The Jacobean Poets*, 1894).

Ars moriendi: a body of Christian literature that emphasises dying well in order to achieve salvation.

It has been suggested that the Duchess is diminished by her premature death in Act IV and that it is Bosola rather than she who is the play's central character. The Duchess' essence is still pervasive after her death, however, both in the haunting echo scene (V.3) and in the other major characters' frequent references to her. Furthermore, the destiny of all the other major characters is determined by her fate and so even if she has less stage time than Bosola, she certainly has a more profound influence. And, of course, she conforms very closely to Aristotle's definition of a tragic hero (see p. 54), whereas Bosola definitely does not!

As a result of her various frailties, Webster makes the Duchess much more credible as a character and thus immensely sympathetic as a tragic heroine. Her stoicism as she maintains her sanity in the face of Ferdinand's best efforts to drive her mad, and her refusal to show fear when Bosola sadistically taunts her with the 'cord' with which she is about to be strangled, are admirable no matter what the complexion of the spectators. Webster's crafting of the Duchess' death scene draws upon both Painter's account and the ***ars moriendi***. As she meets her cruel and undeserved fate with both courage and humility, thus achieving a true pathos that is further intensified by the fact that even the pathologically cynical Bosola appears genuinely impressed, we continue to be awed.

Bosola

In William Painter's account Bosola is merely the assassin, who appears at the end of the story solely in order to murder Antonio. Thus Webster's characterisation of Bosola, unlike that of the Duchess or Antonio, shows considerable inventiveness. Bosola is the play's official malcontent. He is motivated by resentment at society's treatment of him and lives up to his dramatic stereotype by bitterly railing against everyone and everything as he simultaneously pursues his own advancement regardless of any moral considerations. Yet he becomes a far more fascinating and complex character than the traditional malcontent, raising problematic ethical questions about how far he can be blamed for his actions in a society that offers few opportunities for the naturally talented to 'thrive' honestly.

Cynical, resentful and misogynistic, Bosola not only provides much of the play's tension but also allows Webster to present a number of radical social ideas, which the playwright can easily distance himself from owing to Bosola's unsympathetic role as arch-villain. Bosola attacks an entrenched system of patronage, which protects such malevolent oligarchs as the Cardinal and Ferdinand, and which leads to the moral degradation and eventual damnation of those talented individuals whose natural ambition makes them desperate to improve their social status whatever the cost. As such, one can't help but feel that Webster may well be voicing a private concern: 'He and his brother are like plum trees that grow crooked over standing pools…' (I.1). Through this powerfully condensed and highly evocative image, Webster eloquently portrays an unhealthy, undynamic and, therefore, ultimately unproductive society, thus elucidating the enduring truth that corrupt organisations are notoriously inefficient. Of course, Bosola's sole aim is to benefit from such morally questionable patronage: 'Could I be one of their flatt'ring panders, I would hang on their ears like a horse-leech till I were full, and then drop off' (I.1).

(For more on Webster's use of Bosola to express potentially subversive social ideas, see the Nature of nobility and Meritocracy sections of the 'Themes' chapter, p. 24 and p. 25.)

Many critics refer to Bosola's ambiguity. He may not, however, be such an enigma after all. The reality is that there is a fundamental consistency to Bosola – he is utterly contrary. On numerous occasions throughout the play, he deliberately asserts an opposing point of view to the one that has just been presented to him or to the one he knows or suspects that a particular character holds. When Ferdinand asserts that 'great men' have good need to be suspicious, Bosola immediately responds with the seemingly sound advice that suspicion can be counter-productive because it breeds disloyalty. And again, when Ferdinand asserts that any man who could discern his motives would be equally capable of the herculean task of putting a 'girdle' around the world, Bosola responds that Ferdinand flatters himself too much. This time, Ferdinand actually shakes Bosola's hand for this advice, but rather than the plain blunt-speaking good sense that it might appear to be, a close examination of Bosola's conduct throughout the play reveals a pattern of belligerent disagreeability.

Build critical skills

Is Bosola's frequently expressed contempt for sycophants and flatterers based on the fact that he lacks the necessary social skills to ingratiate himself in this way?

Much of this contrariness could be seen as being rooted in the bitterness that arises from his conviction that his talents cannot be honestly employed nor fairly rewarded. Thus, he is utterly unscrupulous and regards his actions not in terms of right or wrong but as entirely justifiable if they serve the cause of his own self-advancement. This is evident when he tells the Cardinal, 'I have done you / Better service than to be slighted thus. / Miserable age, where only the reward / Of doing well is the doing of it.' (I.1). After the murder of the Duchess, we see more of this mindset at work in the face of Ferdinand's failure to reward him. Bosola upbraids Ferdinand for his 'ingratitude' and claims to have 'loathed the evil' but 'loved' the man who commanded it (IV.2). He equates 'doing well' with the efficiency with which he has followed orders and not with the actual nature of the deed.

Build critical skills

How far would you agree that Bosola's relentless evasion of responsibility is reminiscent of the much later defence put up by Nazi war criminals to excuse their horrendous crimes: that they were not morally or legally culpable because they were simply 'following orders'?

Context

The power of the Duchess' death scene is indicated by its influence on later works of fiction, for example, it is referenced in the title of P.D. James' 1962 crime novel *Cover her Face*. The same line also appears in Agatha Christie's 1976 *Sleeping Murder* in which the murderer quotes Ferdinand's words over the body of his victim: 'Cover her face; mine eyes dazzle; she died young'.

The minute Ferdinand has exited after having been 'dazzled' by the sight of his strangled sister, the audience is left in no doubt that Bosola feels no real loyalty to Ferdinand nor, indeed, to anyone. His words are spoken in private and his agenda here as elsewhere is to advance himself by whatever means he can. After Ferdinand's rejection of him because of his heinous role in the murder of the Duchess, Bosola asks himself 'What would I do, were this to do again?' (IV.2). His declaration that he would not exchange his 'peace of conscience / For all the wealth of Europe' is, as is often the case, problematic, since money never seems to have been his main incentive. His motivation, rather, was to gain the status and respect that comes with position. As Webster has Bosola make clear, his corruption 'Grew out of horse dung' (I.1) after Ferdinand offered him the important position of the 'provisorship o'th'horse' in the Duchess' court. It is more his frustration and anger at Ferdinand's refusal to satisfy his desperate need for further enhanced social status that is the catalyst for his sudden attack of conscience, rather than any genuine moral qualms.

When the Duchess appears to revive towards the end of Act IV, Bosola's words should be looked at carefully in the context of all that we know of his character up to this point. He states: 'Her eye opes, / And heaven in it seems to ope, that late was shut, / To take me up to mercy' (IV.2). It sounds like remorse, and the kiss he gives her suggests genuine passion, but his chief focus is still upon his own well-being. He has learned that he has backed the wrong horses with Ferdinand and the Cardinal and suddenly seems concerned that he has damned

CRITICAL VIEW

Psychoanalytic criticism would probably term Bosola a sociopath. You could investigate the characteristics of a sociopath and see how well they apply.

himself in the next world to gain nothing in this one. The Duchess' revival seems therefore to offer a glimmer of hope, not just for her but, more importantly, for himself. He may still be able to save his soul through serving a new master and this he subsequently tries to do in his attempts to help Antonio.

Even if we decide that Bosola is basically self-serving to the end and is unable to take on any responsibility for his own actions, blaming his corruption repeatedly on the brothers, we must not simplify Webster's possible intentions here. The actions and reactions of the characters of the play, just as of people in real life, cannot be divorced from the wider context of the values of the society in which they live. Bosola is a product of his environment. He is an able and pathologically ambitious man for whom his society provides no legitimate channels for advancement. Thus he faces the moral dilemma of whether to be an upright but impoverished non-entity, or a corrupt but potentially upwardly mobile courtier.

At the end of the play, Bosola declares that he 'was an actor in the main of all, / Much 'gainst mine own good nature, yet i'th'end / Neglected' (V.5). As the one-word closing line 'Neglected' perfectly emphasises, his primary reflection is one of self-pity and his reference to his 'own good nature' displays a breath-taking lack of self-knowledge. His dying statement, 'Mine is another voyage', however, does appear to be a recognition of his ultimate moral accountability. This is probably the most sympathetic line given to Bosola. The 'other journey' he refers to is presumably a one-way trip to hell and thus he seems to be acknowledging for the first and only time that his entirely self-interested actions have created considerable harm. It is also possible to ask, though, if there shouldn't be exoneration for the likes of Bosola given the limited choices for one of his birth in this unfair society. Thus, through Bosola, Webster highlights that the ultimate tragedy of the play is as much about the moral failings of an entire social system as it is about the failings of a particular individual.

Antonio

Antonio is closely based on the characterisation to be found in Painter's account of the tragedy, although Webster's Antonio is much less independent in his thinking and much less decisive. At the start of the play, Antonio has recently returned from a long sojourn in the French court and is now employed as the Duchess' steward. This means that he is responsible for her substantial household and thus is overseer of her other employees, including Bosola. Antonio holds quite a privileged position in society and Bosola does comment on his favourable family connections when he remarks that 'a duke was your cousin-german, removed' (II.1). But, of course, Antonio is still an employee and thus in Jacobean eyes of considerably lower status than the Duchess. This is clear when the First Pilgrim asks, 'who would have thought / So great a lady would have matched herself / Unto so mean a person?' (III.4). Ferdinand also refers to him as 'A slave that only smelled of ink and counters, / And ne'er in 's life looked like a gentleman / But in the audit time!' (III.3).

CRITICAL VIEW

A theological reading of the play might liken Bosola's kiss of the Duchess here to the kiss with which Judas betrays Christ in the Garden of Gethsemane. This could enhance the Duchess' Christian martyr-like status, especially as Bosola is clearly identifying the Duchess with salvation.

Build critical skills

A major theme in both Medieval and Renaissance drama is redemption; a key feature of Act V is Bosola's quest for redemption. Why does Webster deny this to him?

CRITICAL VIEW

A Marxist critique might display considerable sympathy for Bosola, deeming his criminality to be the result of restricted opportunity in a rigidly hierarchical and inegalitarian social system.

TASK

Read the synopsis of William Painter's *The Palace of Pleasure* on page 93 and make a list of the similarities and differences between Painter's characterisation of Antonio and Webster's.

Context

In Ancient Greece and Rome, the chorus would consist of a group of actors who provided background or summary information that would help the audience follow the drama.

Build critical skills

Should we view the opening speeches more as an adaptation of the Greek chorus rather than as integral aspects of Antonio's personality?

Taking it further ▶

Search the internet for 'characteristics of Greek tragedy' and more particularly the role of the chorus.

CRITICAL VIEW

A Marxist perspective might highlight the obvious class antagonism here and the threat posed by upwardly mobile bourgeoisie to the long-established aristocratic power, as well as the traditional aristocratic disdain for those whose productivity supports them in their indolent lifestyle.

Antonio is a decent man, but frequently ineffectual, and yet we must be made to believe that this is someone the Duchess would choose to marry despite the great risk to both her reputation and her life. It is wholly significant, therefore, that Webster follows Painter's lead by including in the pre-play jousting the fact that Antonio 'took the ring oft'nest' (I.1). This alludes to his attractive manly physicality, which Painter describes in great detail but which we do not really see Webster present on stage. Webster does, however, have the Duchess suggest Antonio's masculinity when she describes him as 'a complete man' (I.1).

Context

When Webster has the Duchess describe Antonio as 'a complete man', he might well be responding to the popular contempt for the effeminate foppery of many of King James' courtiers. (See the King James' court section of the 'Contexts' chapter, p.65.)

Webster takes great care to establish Antonio as a key figure from the very beginning and his opening speech introduces him as a shrewd political analyst. But there is a question mark here as to whether Webster wrote this speech in order to help develop Antonio's character or if Antonio is simply being used as a choric voice for outlining the play's main political argument, that being that a king moderated by a wise council is a far safer form of government than an absolute monarchy.

The moral and political sentiments expressed, however, are very much in keeping with Antonio's integrity, as is revealed in the rest of the play. Furthermore, the idealism fits well with Antonio's general lack of pragmatism, which frequently exposes him to extreme danger in a world that is governed not by lofty principles but by real politick. It is Antonio who loses the horoscope that he has drawn up for his first son's birth, thus allowing Bosola to provide Ferdinand and the Cardinal with the first piece of vital evidence of the Duchess' defiance of their will. In Act V, it is Antonio's naive belief that he can be reconciled to the Cardinal that results in his death.

Webster also uses Antonio to introduce the play's heroine. The fluent and powerful verse in which Antonio praises the Duchess may veer towards

hyperbole, but his strong feelings for her are clearly evident and thus we can be assured that his acceptance of her proposal of marriage is based on love and not on ambition. The wooing scene puts him at a disadvantage in its reversal of conventional gender roles, of which he himself is only too aware: 'These words should be mine…' (I.1). Perhaps, though, even a modern audience is still too influenced by the lingering patriarchal mores of our own society, which continue to regard men as weak if they do not take the lead in sexual relationships. It is also too easy for us to underestimate Antonio's unease at the social inequality between himself and the Duchess.

The opening of Act III scene 2 shows Antonio at his most sympathetic in its playful wit and relaxed domesticity, and it is clear that even after several years of marriage and the birth of three children, the powerful bond of mutual affection and sexual attraction between the two remains as strong as it was at the beginning of the play.

Antonio inspires love, loyalty and affection, not only in the Duchess but also in Cariola, Delio and Pescara. He ultimately wins Bosola's commendation as 'good Antonio' (V.2 and V.4). Bosola's evident sympathy for the man he previously held in contempt, and his determination to support him in 'a most just revenge' (V.2), significantly expressed in soliloquy and therefore granted the status of honest sincerity, are powerful indicators of Antonio's genuine worth.

Antonio is never given the chance to show his own mettle as a revenger since he does not learn of his wife's murder until he himself is at the point of death. Although he is a skilled jouster and is referred to as 'a soldier' (III.2) by Bosola, again following Painter's lead, Antonio generally displays a severe lack of action in moments of crisis and so appears ineffectual. When he finds Bosola wandering at large in defiance of the general command for all servants to be confined to their quarters in order to conceal the Duchess' sudden labour with their first child, Antonio threatens Bosola that he will 'pull thee up by the roots!' (II.3). This is not backed up by any attempt at physical force, however, and so appears to be no more than empty bluster, which almost farcically results in his own nose suddenly bleeding. When Ferdinand appears unexpectedly in their bedchamber brandishing a dagger and urging the Duchess to commit suicide (III.2), Antonio reappears holding a pistol only *after* Ferdinand has gone – and then he threatens to shoot Cariola!

Antonio's sudden and accidental death at the hands of Bosola, the man who had meant to save him, further serves to diminish him. It smacks of irony and **bathos** and is entirely lacking in grandeur, especially when compared with the tragic **pathos** of the Duchess' fortitude in the face of protracted torture and her stoical demise. Webster does, however, invest Antonio with a dying speech of considerable poetic and philosophical force, in which Antonio reflects on the meaning of life and the futility of ambition ('our quest of greatness'), one of the play's key themes. In this manner, some of his dignity is restored.

Hyperbole: overstatement or elaborate exaggeration.

CRITICAL VIEW

A Marxist critique might well conclude that there is a limit to how much of an influence Antonio can exert on events given the relative disempowerment of the middle classes in Jacobean society.

CRITICAL VIEW

This is the second time that Ferdinand has threatened the Duchess with a poniard. A Freudian interpretation might view this as phallic symbolism, a subconscious expression of Ferdinand's repressed desire to sleep with his sister rather than murder her.

Bathos: anti-climax.
Pathos: a device evoking great pity or sadness.

TASK

Re-read Antonio's speeches in Act I from line 400 and in Act V scene 4 from line 60. Consider what message Webster is trying to impart to his audience regarding ambition.

Perhaps it is because Antonio is such a virtuous and a well-meaning man that he is clearly out of his depth in the murky political world into which he has married. He is a refreshing contrast in that he is wary of ambition, and thus lacks any semblance of the consequent spiritual bankruptcy that we see exhibited not only by Bosola but also by the back-biting officers who relish Antonio's supposed fall from status in Act III scene 2. But perhaps most importantly, by being so ordinary and so human, Antonio enables Webster to portray the Duchess not just as the object of perverse sexual desire who Ferdinand so obsesses over, nor just as a mighty aristocrat, but primarily as a warm human being of 'flesh and blood' (I.1) who is both an adoring wife and a loving mother.

The Cardinal

Webster's Cardinal is clearly based on Painter's characterisation. Webster borrows such details as his and his younger brother's joint use of political power to make the Duchess and her family stateless, and the detail of having many years earlier ordered a cold-blooded assassination of what Painter describes as 'a poore Gentleman which neuer thought him hurt.' Though just as furious as his brother over the Duchess' disobedience, Painter's Cardinal uses much more moderate language.

Apart from a brief return to Catholicism under Mary I, England had been a Protestant country since Henry VIII's break with the Roman Catholic Church in the 1530s (although Henry was only politically Protestant, and still persecuted radical Protestants). *The Duchess of Malfi* was first performed in 1614. Thus the character of the Cardinal might be viewed as an attack on Catholicism. (For more on this, see the Religion section in the 'Contexts' chapter, p. 71.) Webster's characterisation of the Cardinal, however, can also stand more generally as an indictment of the hypocrisy, worldliness and corruption of supposedly devout churchmen anywhere.

Just as Bosola is the malcontent, the Cardinal fulfils another stereotypical role in the drama of the period, that of the machiavel. As such, he embodies most of the expected features of the outwardly composed politician who manipulates others to his own ends through devious and ruthless machinations, while his cool exterior is merely a front for the murder and treachery that he perceives as essential to his own self-advancement. Just like Bosola, however, by the end of the play he has transcended the stereotype, although perhaps not to the same degree.

As with his sister, he is known only by his title, which is heavily ironic because, as Webster has Bosola establish right at the beginning of the play, the Cardinal is far from holy: 'Some fellows, they say, are possessed with the devil, but this great fellow were able to possess the greatest devil and make him worse' (I.1).

In Act I, Antonio gives an account of the Cardinal as a corrupt politician who has unsuccessfully attempted to bribe his way into the position of Pope. This is particularly revealing about the Cardinal's primary focus being on worldly power rather than on spiritual affairs. Although ostensibly an eminent man, he is typical of any ordinary courtier in that he suffers from the play's all-too-common ailment, ambition. It is this obsession with self-advancement and status that makes him as firmly opposed to his sister's remarrying as is Ferdinand, but without his brother's repressed sexual jealousy. As far as the Cardinal is concerned, Bosola's discovery of the Duchess having given birth is primarily an offence against family honour: **'Shall our blood, / The royal blood of Aragon and Castile, / Be thus attainted?'** (II.5).

Top ten quotation

But the sin of pride is far from the Cardinal's only moral transgression. In Act I Delio tells us that, seven years earlier, the Cardinal had employed Bosola to assassinate an opponent, and then callously betrayed his agent by allowing him to be condemned to hard labour during the intervening period. An additional sin to the Cardinal's discredit is his lust, which is exemplified in his gloating participation in an adulterous relationship with Julia, thus scorning the holy sanctity of marriage. In Act II scene 4 we see him arrogantly belittling Julia for her infidelity and cruelly joking that she will never be able to make a cuckold of him because, with his assistance, she is already actively cuckolding her elderly husband, Castruchio.

The second, and final, time that we find the Cardinal alone with Julia is in Act V scene 2, and here Webster displays the Cardinal at his most nefarious. Initially, the Cardinal reveals that he ordered the strangling of the Duchess and two of her children. He then follows this startlingly cold-blooded revelation by murdering Julia in a most premeditated fashion, not because of the dangerous secret that he has just entrusted to her but simply because he has grown 'weary of her and by any means / Would be quit off' (V.2).

Through use of the poisoned Bible to dispatch Julia, Webster employs the most powerful symbol at his disposal to demonstrate the depth of this character's moral degradation, while simultaneously emphasising just how far removed this supposed cleric is from God. This is the only time in the play when we see the Cardinal actually 'get his hands dirty' and thus finally begin to transcend the machiavel stereotype. It would seem safe to assume that there is a very personal motivation for him to take such a risk in murdering Julia and, therefore, her murder is of a very different ilk to the other murders, which have been coolly commissioned and which, presumably, were more strategically motivated.

Given the sinful nature of this character, it is with considerable relish that Webster finally invests the normally emotionally detached Cardinal with genuine passion when at the beginning of Act V scene 5 he ponders the nature of the 'one material fire' in hell. This beautifully crafted poetry encapsulates the Cardinal's sense of foreboding that his life is near its end, and as a result his thoughts drift to the next life, in which the only possible outcome is eternal damnation. The vividly expressed terror in this speech is clearly a warning to all ruthless and self-promoting individuals.

The Cardinal's political influence has already been demonstrated in his power to 'solicit the state of Ancona' (III.3) to deny asylum to the Duchess and Antonio and, prior to becoming a high-ranking cleric, the Cardinal was a military commander of considerable repute. When the Cardinal asks 'Must we turn soldier then?', Malateste responds that the Emperor has heard of 'your worth that way…' (III.3). Webster, however, ensures that any dignity that this might afford the Cardinal is fully stripped away from him by the end of the play. Thus when Bosola announces his intention to kill the Cardinal, the Cardinal's response is blatantly craven, 'My dukedom, for rescue!' (V.5). In this way, his death is genuinely ignoble, especially in terms of the *ars moriendi*. Webster does not even allow the Cardinal any grand dying speech and further assures the audience of his ultimate insignificance: '… let me / Be laid by, and never thought of' (V.5).

It is left to Delio to underscore the play's main moral message when he alludes to the pointless folly of such a life, dedicated to the ruthless pursuit of worldly self-advancement: 'These wretched eminent things / Leave no more fame behind 'em than should one / Fall in a frost and leave his print in snow…' (V.5). Thus although the Cardinal does largely conform to the narrow dramatic stereotype of the ruthless machiavel, his immoral life and inglorious death take on a much greater significance when viewed in terms of the play's moral subtext.

Ferdinand

Webster creates enormous dramatic interest through the contrast between the two brothers, in which Ferdinand is as intemperate as the Cardinal is self-controlled. Again, the main source is Painter. In *The Palace of Pleasure*, the unnamed younger brother's reaction to the news that the Duchess has married Antonio is particularly lengthy and vituperative, for example 'I wil make ye daunce sutch a bloudy **bargenet**, as your whorish heate for euer shall be cooled.' Of the Cardinal, however, Painter writes 'The cardinal also was out of quiet, grinding his teeth together…'

Bargenette: a type of dance.

Just as Webster's Cardinal can be viewed as representative of a corrupt Church that is focused more on temporal power than on spiritual matters, Ferdinand can be viewed as representing the corruption of another of the fundamental pillars of society: the law. When Antonio describes Ferdinand's predatory practices as a magistrate, Delio responds with the conclusion that 'the law to him / Is like a foul black cobweb to a spider, / He makes it his dwelling, and a prison / To entangle those shall feed him' (I.1). Rather than an instrument of justice, the law has become a tool of oppression employed by the rich and powerful in order to control and exploit those lower down the social order.

CRITICAL VIEW

Once again, this character lends itself to a Marxist interpretation through its possible presentation of economic exploitation and class conflict.

Of course, any discussion on Ferdinand must perforce consider his relationship with his twin sister, the iridescent Duchess. Although it is never made explicit, Ferdinand's underlying motivation seems to be a suppressed incestuous desire, and this is a feature of his character that definitely does not appear in Painter's account. Antonio describes Ferdinand's 'perverse and turbulent nature' (I.1) and this is particularly evident in his passionate injunction to his sister not to remarry. This is couched in an obsession with her sexuality as he refers to 'lustful pleasures' (I.1) and warns her against the temptation of being seduced by 'a neat knave with a smooth tale' (I.1).

CRITICAL VIEW

Frank Whigham disputes the view that Ferdinand harbours an incestuous sexual desire towards his sister, regarding Ferdinand's reaction to the Duchess' marriage to Antonio as a terror of social impurity: 'Ferdinand's incestuous inclination toward his sister is a social posture, of hysterical compensation – a desperate expression of the desire to evade degrading association with inferiors' (*Incest and Ideology*, 1985).

Context

```
Bertolt Brecht opened his 1946 adaptation of The Duchess of
Malfi with a prologue borrowed from the opening scene of
John Ford's 'Tis Pity She's a Whore (1633), which includes
the lines 'Shall, then, for that I am her brother born,
/ My joys be ever banished from her bed?' This addition
clearly establishes Ferdinand's obsession with the Duchess
as incestuous.
```

▲ Portrait of Richard Burbage (1567–1619), a contemporary actor who played Ferdinand

As one might expect, Ferdinand's response to Bosola's communication that his sister has given birth completely overlooks the maternal significance of the event. Instead, he launches into a series of lurid sexual fantasies as he imagines his sister engaging in unrestrained promiscuity with such social non-entities as 'some strong-thighed bargeman; / Or one o'th'woodyard that can quoit the sledge…' (II.5). He follows this with an even more disturbing sado-sexual streak as he conjures up such grotesquely extravagant scenarios as: himself drinking the Duchess' blood rather than her 'whore's milk'; burning her and her lover alive in their bed sheets; and boiling 'their bastard to a **cullis**', which he will then feed to the child's father in order to revitalise the latter's energy so that he can resume fornicating with his sister. Ferdinand does eventually manage to compose himself and postpone his desire to act upon his consuming sexual jealousy long enough for the Duchess to give birth to two more children. It is clear, though, that his sanity is in danger of slipping, so much so that the Cardinal pointedly asks him, 'Are you stark mad?' (II.5).

Cullis: a meat broth.

As to why Webster leaves an approximate period of two years before Ferdinand enacts vengeance, one might be advised once again to focus on plot development rather than character development. Webster is closely following Painter's account, which describes how the brothers – although incensed – delayed their revenge in order 'to know the lucky Louer that had so wel tilled the Duchesse their Sister's field'. Secondly, Webster's presentation of Ferdinand's fury is electrifying, and even more intense than Painter's, but if he were to allow Ferdinand to act suddenly upon his violent impulses, the play would finish at least one act too early! Thus Webster excuses the delay by having Ferdinand assure the Cardinal that 'Till I know who leaps my sister, I'll not stir' (II.5).

When Ferdinand finally does take his revenge in Act IV, it is gratuitously gruesome and macabre. It is Ferdinand's express desire that before the Duchess is killed, she is to be driven insane. Webster has fashioned a darkly poetic intensity here because

Build critical skills

Is there any evidence to support Ferdinand's explanation to Bosola that the reason behind his ferocious vendetta against the Duchess is because 'I had a hope – / Had she continued widow – to have gained / An infinite mass of treasure by her death…' (IV.2)?

CRITICAL VIEW

Modern psychoanalytic criticism could clearly interpret Ferdinand's wolf-like behaviour as sexually predatory and as indicative of a dissociative personality disorder.

CRITICAL VIEW

'Webster … adopts the romantic convention that men are, in the second of death, most essentially and significantly themselves' (Rupert Brooke, *John Webster and the Elizabethan Drama*, 1916).

Ferdinand may well sense that her 'betrayal' of him has cost him his sanity – which, indeed, it has. Thus he maliciously afflicts her with a dead man's severed hand and with a waxwork display that purports to show the corpses of Antonio and their children, and then he follows this by subjecting her to the babbling of the 'mad folk' from the 'common hospital' so as to deprive her of sleep. Even the relentless Bosola appears to be disturbed by the extreme nature of the punishment and urges Ferdinand to 'go no farther in your cruelty' (IV.1). Ferdinand's reply says it all: 'Damn her, that body of hers…'

Ultimately, the only way he seems able to cope with the psychological pain of the immense rejection that he experiences as a result of the Duchess' remarriage, is to destroy her. His sudden change of heart after seeing her strangled body, blaming Bosola for not saving her, however, is typically perverse. His passing references to wolves augur his own imagined transformation into one and thus his descent into lycanthropia is well foreshadowed: 'The wolf shall find her grave and scrape it up' (IV.2) and 'I'll go hunt the badger, by owl-light' (IV.2). The first of these allusions reappears in the context of the knockabout comedy that surrounds the Doctor in Act V scene 2. Ferdinand is described as having dug up 'the leg of a man' (V.2) in a churchyard in what is a poignant moment of genuine tragi-comedy: on one level his behaviour is sacrilegious and undignified, though certainly ludicrous; on another level, if Ferdinand was searching for the corpse of his departed sister, then there is a genuine pathos here.

Throughout Act V, Ferdinand is clinically insane, fantasising about driving snails to Moscow as a test of patience (V.2), or about participating in the military action he had craved at the start of the play (V.5). Only at the point of death does he regain some semblance of sanity, his dying sententia recognising the truth that his downfall is self-inflicted: 'Whether we fall by ambition, blood, or lust, / Like diamonds we are cut with our own dust' (V.5). As is often the case, Webster uses a major character's final words in order to express a profound moral or philosophical insight.

As tempting as it might be to pronounce upon Ferdinand with the benefit of modern psychology, it is also important firstly to consider his slide into insanity from a Jacobean perspective. As we see in Shakespeare's plays *Hamlet*, *Macbeth* and *King Lear*, there was definitely an awareness of madness as a medical condition brought about by trauma. Despite being a firm believer in the existence of witches, even King James inclined towards a medical diagnosis of lycanthropia in his treatise on supernatural evil, *Daemonologie* (1597), deeming it to arise from 'melancholie'. By this he was referring to a mental illness in Jacobean 'humour psychology', which was the belief that an imbalance in the bodily fluids (the humours) could create an imbalance in the mind:

> *There hath indeede bene an old opinion of such like things … men-woolfes. But to tell you simplie my opinion in this, if anie such thing hath bene, I take it to haue proceeded but of a naturall super-abundance of Melancholie, which as wee reade, that it hath made some thinke themselues Pitchers, and some horses, and some one kinde of beast or other…*

(*Daemonologie*, 1597)

Webster, of course, has Ferdinand treated by a doctor and not by a priest. The Jacobean attitude to madness, however, is complicated by the religious beliefs of the time, by which madness could also be viewed as a form of demonic possession and could certainly be seen as a punishment for sin.

There are several references made by various characters that connect Ferdinand with Satan, especially the grimly humorous retort by Malateste when Roderigo comments on the wildness of the storm that seemed to shake Ferdinand's chamber: ''Twas nothing but pure kindness in the devil / To rock his own child' (V.4). Despite the many references to the supernatural, however, the evil that Webster presents is essentially human in origin and arises not from demonic intervention, as we see in Marlowe's *Dr Faustus* or Shakespeare's *Macbeth*, but out of a misgoverned society. Thus, when considering the origin of Ferdinand's illness, Webster's presentation largely accords with that of King James, even to the extent that Ferdinand also imagines himself to be a horse: 'Give me some wet hay, I am broken winded' (V.5).

It is Edward Grimestone's 1607 translation of Simon Goulart's *Admirable and Memorable Histories of Our Time*, however, that appears to be the main source for Ferdinand's lycanthropia. Grimestone, like King James, views the illness as a 'melancholike humor' and describes sufferers running through churchyards at night, robbing graves; he describes one man in particular who 'carried then vpon his shoulders the whole thigh and the legge of a dead man.' Of another lycanthrope, he notes the man's remark 'that Wolues were commonlie hayrie [hairy] without, and hee was betwixt the skinne and the flesh.'

Certainly, Ferdinand's madness can be viewed from a theological perspective in terms of it being a punishment for his many egregious misdemeanours. Equally, though, it can be regarded as a perceptive analysis of a complete psychotic break with reality brought about by the trauma of having committed a crime so heinous that he can no longer bear to live with the knowledge of what he has done. This unbearable torment is further compounded by his overwhelming grief over the loss of the woman with whom he had so long been obsessed. As he correctly diagnoses in his dying speech, 'My sister! Oh my sister, there's the cause on 't!' (V.5).

Delio

In Painter's *The Palace of Pleasure*, Delio appears only very briefly at the end of the tale in the guise of a well-meaning stranger who comes to warn Antonio of an assassination plot against him and, more tragically, to inform Antonio of the Duchess's violent death whilst in prison. Webster expands Delio's role quite considerably, making him the loyal friend and confidante. In this respect, he is a familiar dramatic stereotype, another notable example being Horatio in *Hamlet*. In some ways, Delio acts as the audience's representative, offering a convenient ear for information vital to the understanding of the spectators, from Antonio's character sketches of the Duchess and her brothers to his regular updates on the progress of events. Indeed, the play is partly structured around Delio's

Taking it further

Research the 'Jacobean theory of humours' online and write a brief description of each of the supposed four humours/temperaments.

Context

George Gifford, writing a few years prior to King James, declared in his *A Dialogue Concerning Witches and Witchcrafts* (1593), 'These divels make the witches in some places believe, that they are turned into the likenesse of wolves...'

conversations with Antonio which begin Acts I, III and V. Delio is also central to the play's denouement as it is he who promotes the succession of Antonio's son to the dukedom. However, despite all of Delio's integrity and sound advice, Webster compromises him in Act II, scene 2 when he reveals that Delio is one of Julia's former suitors and has him attempt to purchase her sexual favours.

Julia

Julia is Webster's own invention. She is largely stereotyped as the embodiment of transgressive female lust, a 'strumpet' in Pescara's words (V.1), but she is not portrayed unsympathetically. She is seen partly as a victim of patriarchal power, whether through being saddled with an old and impotent husband or through being subjected to the lascivious desires of a powerful politician, the Cardinal. However, she is proactive and so effectively uses her seductive skills for her own ends. As a woman who has chosen one particular means of achieving success in a masculine world, Julia ends up being destroyed by a deeply misogynistic and patriarchal society that will only accept women who ultimately conform to male requirements.

Cariola

Cariola is very closely modelled on Painter's unnamed 'Gentlewoman which had ben brought up with her [The Duchess] from the cradle, and was made priuy to the heauy mariage of those two louers which was consummate in hir presence.' Her role frequently parallels that of Delio in respect of being a confidante. However, unlike Delio, she is a servant and thus her sound advice is easily dismissed, for example, when she warns the Duchess against pursuing Bosola's suggestion of a feigned pilgrimage to Loreto in Act III, scene 2. Webster makes great dramatic use of her in the Duchess's death scene in which her terrified pleading for her life, even to the extent of falsely claiming that she is 'quick with child' (IV.2), contrasts powerfully with the Duchess's noble stoicism.

Castruchio

In Painter's *The Palace of Pleasure*, there is an Alfonso Castruccio who is the Cardinal of Siena, a politically powerful figure who assists the Aragonian brothers by having the Duchess and her family banished from his city. However, Webster's representation heavily puns upon the character's surname, which sounds very much like castrato, a male singer castrated in boyhood so as to main his soprano or alto voice. Consequently, Webster's Castruchio is a sexually impotent figure who is regularly cuckolded by the sexually rapacious Julia. He is a figure of fun to be scorned by other characters for the audience's delight. His main importance lies in the fact that he is quite clearly meant to satisfy the popular contemporary contempt at the perceived inferior quality of King James' courtiers who were generally regarded as both self-serving and effeminate. Webster's intention here is particularly apparent at the beginning of Act II, scene 1 when Bosola satirically advises Castruchio as to how to be 'taken for an eminent courtier'.

Target your thinking

- How does Webster develop his themes, settings and characters as the dramatic action unfolds? (**AO1**)
- What dramatic methods does Webster use to shape the audience's responses at crucial points in the play? (**AO2**)

Form

Principally, a play is written to be performed; it is meant to be a spectacle. A performance is far more direct and multisensory than when we simply read the script. Theatre audiences are meant to be exposed to the presence of professional actors who have a mastery of dialogue, expression, gesture and movement. In addition, there is the enthralling impact of costume, scenery, lighting, sudden plunges into darkness, music and the additional psychological dimension of being part of a group dynamic. If it is not possible to see the play performed exactly as the author originally intended, as is the case with any Jacobean drama, then readers have to fall back on the script because that is what is left to them. Characterisation, action, settings, the language of the play and, of course, the stage directions can all provide us with clues to inform possible interpretations.

In *The Duchess of Malfi*, there are fewer stage directions than we would find in a modern drama; this was the norm for play scripts from this period. As a consequence, this leaves considerable scope for a director (and a modern editor!) to interpret how best to convey the play. Having said that, there are still many clear indications within the script as to how Webster wished particular scenes to be staged, and this could be part of your focus when responding to an examination question regarding Webster's intentions.

Thus, you might consider elements such as:

- ◤ The impact of the entrances and exits, such as in Act III scene 2 when Antonio comes out of hiding holding a pistol only *after* Ferdinand has disappeared, which makes him appear distinctly unheroic. Similarly, the impact of Bosola's sudden entrance in Act V scene 5 immediately after the Cardinal has related his terrifying vision of seeing 'a thing armed with a rake / That seems to strike at me' (V.5), the effect of which is clearly to create excitement by dramatically foreshadowing forthcoming events.

- ◤ The use of other stage directions, such as the explicit instruction regarding the use of light and darkness in Act IV scene 1 when Ferdinand deceives his sister with the severed hand. The impact of this is to contribute to the sense

Context

In the 1623 first published edition of the play, the names of all participating characters were grouped at the beginning of each scene and so modern editors have had to locate exits and entrances at points that seem most appropriate to them.

of hopeless gloom, create suspense, make Ferdinand's deception credible, and create empathy and pathos for the Duchess by simultaneously shocking the audience with the sudden exposure of the horrifying hand.

▼ The use of props such as the waxworks, which is clearly indicated in the stage direction in Act IV scene 1: 'Here is discovered behind a traverse the artificial figures of ANTONIO and his children, appearing as if they were dead'. This is clearly visually electrifying and simultaneously contributes considerable impact to the overwhelming sense of evil that pervades the latter part of the play.

You might also consider the impact of the dramatic features that were an integral part of theatre at the time when Webster was writing:

▼ The dumb show in Act III scene 4, in which the Cardinal is invested with his new military status and the Duchess, Antonio and their children are banished, for which Webster has provided fairly detailed stage directions. The overall effect is to convey with considerable theatrical force the great increase in the Cardinal's power, thus making the Duchess' sudden fall seem even more perilous.

▼ The 'ditty ... sung to very solemn music, by divers churchmen' during the above ceremony, which 'the author disclaims'. It nevertheless has a considerable impact on the audience as it overwhelms their auditory sense with rapturous praise for the Cardinal in his new role as warrior general, yet again emphasising the comparative weakness and extreme vulnerability of the now-powerless Duchess and her family.

▼ The song set to 'a dismal kind of music' in Act IV scene 2, which produces an appropriately brooding atmosphere through its both sonic and lyrical discordancy. This foreshadows Ferdinand's total mental collapse into lycanthropia with its opening line, 'Oh let us howl'.

▼ The antimasque of the madmen in the same scene, which is intended to introduce some appropriately grim comic relief so as to provide a brief respite from the tension. This may also symbolically represent the general 'madness' and chaos of such a badly managed society, and the consequent immense frustrations of the emergent middle class, as is suggested by the fact that such key social figures as a lawyer, a priest, a doctor and an astrologist are included in the line-up.

Above all, the essential ingredient of great drama is conflict, so when studying the play script look out for the many conflicts that Webster has deliberately created in order to generate the suspense necessary for carrying his audience through to the denouement.

Renaissance versus medieval drama

From the fourteenth to the sixteenth centuries, Classical humanism became an unstoppable intellectual force throughout Western Europe. This period has become known as the Renaissance and one of its presiding characteristics was a revival of interest in the cultures of Ancient Greece and Rome. This resulted in a revolution in thought and ushered in great advances in such areas as science, technology, philosophy, literature, architecture and art. There was also considerable expansion in business, commerce and international exploration.

By the late sixteenth and early seventeenth centuries, when Webster and Shakespeare were writing, a new type of drama had been established. This was clearly influenced by Classical models and was significantly more sophisticated than the medieval plays that had preceded it. Ten of the major developments include:

- An overall structure that is clearly influenced by the great dramatists of Ancient Greece and Rome, especially Seneca.

- Much longer and infinitely more complex plays, often with highly sophisticated use of subplot or double plot.

- A shift of focus from a theocentric universe to one in which mankind literally takes centre stage. Thus, for example, the tension between good and evil becomes a driving force in human psychology rather than primarily a supernatural encounter.

- A presentation of a world in which God's order is often much less apparent than had been the case in medieval drama.

- A consequent focus on man's capacity for creating chaos and upon the survivors' struggle to restore order.

- An exploration of relationships between individuals, and between individuals and society, rather than just between man and God.

- A much greater emphasis on secular themes such as society, politics, money, romance and human sexuality, although religion still remained an extremely important element.

- A focus on universal human problems, which makes Renaissance drama still so relevant today, especially the exploration of the tension between desire and moral or social responsibility.

- Fully realised characters with extremely sophisticated psychology, as opposed to the two-dimensional characters of medieval drama who might, for example, simply represent a single vice or virtue.

- An emphasis on providing entertainment rather than just religious or moral instruction.

There were also, linked to these, certain practical developments: the rise of professional acting companies; the emergence of writers with shareholders and financial backers; the construction of purpose-built theatres; the rise of a mass audience drawn from all social strata.

When considering the form, structure and language of the plays written during this period, you should recognise that without the Renaissance this exciting and incredibly sophisticated new form of drama could not have arisen.

TASK

Discuss the ways in which Webster's play meets the criteria in this list.

Taking it further ▶

The Renaissance is a huge topic and its influence can still be felt today. You might wish to research it further online.

Aristotelian Tragedy

In his *Poetics,* Aristotle (384BCE–322BCE) defined the two most important elements in tragedy as being plot and character, and explained that the purpose of tragedy was to provide catharsis. The audience would find healthful emotional release through observing 'incidents arousing pity and fear'. In order for this civilising psychological purge to take place, Aristotle argued that the hero should be 'a man who is highly renowned and prosperous, but one who is not pre-eminently virtuous and just, whose misfortune, however, is brought upon him not by vice or depravity but by some error of judgement or frailty...'

Aristotle terms this 'hamartia'. The Duchess' hamartia is that she succumbs to a young woman's desire for romantic love and so places personal happiness above duty. This is much more an error of judgement than a serious moral flaw. Aristotle writes that our 'pity is aroused by unmerited misfortune, fear by the misfortune of a man like ourselves.' This 'unmerited misfortune', the tragedy, will arise out of the climactic interaction between the hero's hamartia and unkind circumstance dictated by fate (or the will of the gods).

Context

The influence of Classical drama during the Jacobean period can be discerned from the playwright John Ford's commendatory verse to the 1623 first published edition of *The Duchess of Malfi*: 'Crown him a poet, whom nor Rome, nor Greece, / Transcend in all theirs, for a masterpiece...'

The influence of Seneca

Webster's characterisation of the Duchess very accurately conforms to Aristotle's definition (see above), in that she deserves so much better than she receives and she is *so* recognisably human. Most critics, however, agree that Webster and the other dramatists of the period were more directly influenced by tragedies written nearly four centuries after Aristotle, by the Roman dramatist Seneca (4BCE–AD65). In 1589, the playwright, poet and pamphleteer Thomas Nash observed: 'yet English Seneca read by candle light yeeldes manie good sentences ... he will affoord you whole Hamlets, I should say handfulls of tragical speaches.' Webster even reveals his own familiarity with Seneca when he has Bosola declare near the beginning of the play, 'What creature ever fed worse than hoping Tantalus?' (I.1), Tantalus being the character who opens Seneca's classic revenge drama, *Thyestes*.

Most critics believe that Seneca's tragedies are meant to be recited rather than performed. The characteristics of Senecan tragedy are:

- a division into five parts
- blank verse and much use of metaphorical language
- a chorus, which provides essential background information and which comments upon the action
- long reflective soliloquies
- sententious philosophy and moral maxims
- a morally indifferent universe
- stoicism and a sense of hopeless fatalism
- ghosts
- sexual transgression and obsessive desire
- detailed accounts of horror and violence
- revenge and deceit as central themes
- a bloody denouement.

Referring to the work of John Marston, Cyril Tourneur and Webster, L.G. Salingar remarks, 'like most drama of the time, it draws heavily from Seneca, by way of Kyd and his *Spanish Tragedy* (c.1589) – both Seneca the moral sage and Seneca the fabricator of ghastly revenges' ('Tourneur and the Tragedy of Revenge' in *The Pelican Guide to English Literature, Volume 2*, 1963). Although Seneca was plainly a great influence on Elizabethan and Jacobean dramatists, by adopting aspects of Seneca's style these dramatists were also clearly influencing each other. (For more on the key form of Jacobean revenge tragedy see pages 33–5 of this guide.)

Structure

The dramatic arc

When we talk about the structure of a play, we mean the manner in which it has been constructed. *The Duchess of Malfi* has often been criticised for its apparently 'random' structure and for its collapse into anti-climax after the Duchess' death. Webster's departure from the norm, however, could instead be regarded as both radical and courageous.

From the title, it is clear that the play's central character is meant to be the Duchess. There is the danger, though, that by having her killed in Act IV Webster deflects attention from her in his departure from the conventional use of the five-act structure. Although Webster and his contemporaries did not subdivide their dramas into five acts, this having been done by editors and publishers at a later date, they were conforming to a five-part structure originally advocated by the Roman poet and literary critic Horace (65–8BCE) in his *Ars Poetica*, which

▲ Lucius Annaeus Seneca, or Seneca the Younger, c.4BCE–AD65

went on to influence Seneca. The German author and literary critic Gustav
Freytag (1816–95), having analysed Classical and Renaissance drama, noted a
commonality of structure that did indeed break down into five distinctive phases.
As a result, he developed a brilliant analytical tool that is sometimes referred to
as the 'dramatic arc':

- **Exposition:** the main characters are introduced and any necessary
  background information is provided so as to set the scene for later events.
- **Rising action:** these are the events that occur after the exposition and, as
  a result of a complication or conflict, they create rising tension and so power
  the play through to its climax.
- **Climax (or crisis):** this is the main turning-point in the story, in which an
  event takes place that will drastically alter the protagonist's fate. In the
  case of tragedy, this will be the beginning of a catastrophic decline in the
  protagonist's fortunes.
- **Falling action:** the conflict between the protagonist and antagonist
  becomes fully exposed and at the end of the act, the ultimate outcome is still
  in doubt, hence generating a considerable degree of suspense.
- **Denouement (or catastrophe):** the conflict culminates and, in a tragedy,
  this generally results in the death of the hero or heroine and a great deal of
  fall-out for those around him/her.

It is artificial to apply the above formula too precisely to the division into acts of
any Elizabethan or Jacobean play because those divisions were not created by
the dramatists of the day. Nonetheless, these playwrights were educated men
who were well versed in the ideas and writings of the ancients. Webster's play
clearly does largely conform to Freytag's dramatic arc – but with the notable
exception that the heroine dies at the end of Act IV, and not Act V!

So, does this add to or detract from the success of the play as a whole? Well,
the Duchess' premature death certainly dominates the rest of the action. It
generates enormous suspense and one can honestly say that the conflict set up
in the falling action is not fully resolved until the audience's thirst to see justice
done has been satisfied by the end of the play, at which point all of the Duchess'
antagonists have gained exactly what they deserve.

Parallel scenes

Another interesting structural aspect of the play is Webster's use of parallel
scenes. For example, the abortive affair between Julia and Bosola parodies
the genuine love story of the Duchess and Antonio. Julia too woos and 'wins'
Bosola, but here it is a matter of unabashed lust. As Julia states, 'Now you'll
say / I am wanton; this nice modesty in ladies / Is but a troublesome familiar /
That haunts them' (V.2). This contrasts with the Duchess' bashful confession

of her love for Antonio: 'Oh, let me shroud my blushes in your bosom' (I.1). Bosola's response is to accept Julia's advances, just as Antonio accepts those of the Duchess. Bosola's purpose, though, as we learn in an aside, is to 'work upon this creature' (V.2) to help him gain information from her other lover, the Cardinal. These events all mirror the earlier scene of the Duchess and Antonio, offering a clear contrast between pure, selfless love and the unbridled lust of the entirely self-motivated. Ironically, Webster shows the outcome to be the same for all, thus 'proving' the thesis introduced in the opening speech of the play that any corruption at the 'head' of the fountain will rain down destruction on all, regardless of whom they are or what they represent.

A second example of this technique of parallel scenes is when Webster has the Cardinal confine everyone to their room in Act V scene 4 so that he can conceal his murder of Julia and the intended murders of Antonio and Bosola. This mirrors Act II scene 2 where Antonio, acting on Delio's advice, has concocted a strategic lie in order to keep everyone in their chambers throughout the night so as to hide the Duchess' labour. Again, we are dealing with polar opposites, this time between birth and death.

As well as providing a satisfying aesthetic, such plotting creates a sense of déjà vu and thus reinforces the strong sense of fatalism within the play.

Horror and violence

Writing in 1898, George Bernard Shaw harshly condemns 'the opacity that prevented Webster, the Tussaud laureate, from appreciating his own stupidity…' In his poem 'Whispers of Immortality', published in 1918, the year in which the brutal carnage of World War I finally ended, T.S. Eliot remarks: 'Webster was much possessed by death / And saw the skull beneath the skin'. Writing in 1924 in his essay 'Four Elizabethan Dramatists', however, Eliot is far more effusive about Webster's literary merit, if not about his vision: '*The Duchess of Malfi* will provide an interesting example of a very great literary and dramatic genius directed towards chaos.'

Extreme horror and violence are definitely aspects of Webster's style but they are also integral features in other classic 'revenge tragedies'. Rather than the crass sensationalism and cheap thrills that Shaw perceives, or the nihilistic disorder to which Eliot alludes, others see a deeply moral intent. According to this interpretation, Webster graphically displays human nature at its worst while simultaneously portraying the inevitably tragic outcome of such behaviour, both on the Earth plane and in the next. Aristocrat and English literature professor Lord David Cecil, for example, views Webster's drama as 'a study of the working of sin in the world' in the context of 'the supremacy of that Divine Law against which they have offended' (*Poets and Storytellers*, 1949).

Build critical skills

To what extent is the presentation of a world progressively spiralling into chaos an essential element of tragedy?

CRITICAL VIEW

'Though earnest critics have tried to present him as a Christian moralist, a proto-feminist and even a daring existentialist, what clearly turned Webster on was cruelty.' (Charles Spencer, theatre critic for *The Telegraph*, reviewing a 2003 production of the play at the National Theatre starring Janet McTeer).

CRITICAL VIEW

'If we present a tragedy we include the fatal and abortive ends of such as commit notorious murders … to terrify men from like abhorred practices' (Thomas Heywood, *An Apology for Actors*, 1612).

Build critical skills

Consider whether great literature must always have a moral purpose. Must moral literature always have an unambiguous conclusion?

CRITICAL VIEW

'Life, as it appears to Webster, is a moral chaos. Ultimately no clarifying philosophy is possible.' (Travis Bogard, *The Tragic Satire of John Webster*, 1955).

CRITICAL VIEW

'In Webster's plays, salvation and damnation are ever-present realities.' (David Gunby, *John Webster: Three Plays*, 1972).

Build critical skills

Gamini Salgado refers to 'the revival of a medieval notion that the world was running down and civilisation on the brink of destruction' (*Three Jacobean Tragedies*, 1985). Do we see any evidence of this in Webster's play?

Black comedy

There is also the thorny issue of humour in the horror scenes. In terms of the plot, the function of the madmen in Act IV scene 2 is deadly serious. Here, Ferdinand's intention is to advance the destruction of his sister's sanity by depriving her of sleep: 'let them practise together, sing and dance / And act their gambols to the full o'th'moon' (IV.1). Webster may also, however, have designed their ludicrous ramblings to amuse, by tapping into the popular contemporary public pastime of seeking entertainment by observing the mentally ill inmates in London's Bethlem Royal Hospital ('Bedlam'). Of course, to a modern sensibility this is crass insensitivity.

Build critical skills

Travis Bogard appears to see Webster's worldview as nihilistic, i.e. that life is ultimately bleak and pointless, whereas David Gunby argues that Webster writes from a deeply Christian perspective in which life is a test of one's moral character. What do you think?

There are, though, aspects of Ferdinand's own insane antics that are genuinely comical even today, e.g. the Doctor's line that 'he howled fearfully; / Said he was a wolf, only the difference / Was, a wolf's skin was hairy on the outside, / His on the inside' (V.2). Equally humorous is the doctor's over-confident assertion that he will 'buffet his madness out of him', only then to be thrown to the ground and pummelled himself:

> PESCARA. Doctor, he did not fear you throughly.
> DOCTOR. True, I was somewhat too forward.

(V.2)

But as Dominic Dromgoole's four-hundred-year-anniversary 2014 production of the play at the Sam Wanamaker Playhouse, Shakespeare's Globe, proves, the audience reaction to some of the more extreme gruesomeness can be problematic. Writing for the *Times Higher Education* website, Liz Schafer's review of the performance includes the following observation:

The sometimes confrontational intimacy of the playhouse may be one reason why this Duchess of Malfi generated a lot of laughs. Waxworks, a dead man's hand, a reviving corpse, a poisonous book, lycanthropy and a pile of corpses – some aspects of The Duchess are always going to seem borderline Hammer House of Horror. But although some of the laughter arose from embarrassment and shock, laughter is itself under scrutiny in this play.

(www.timeshighereducation.com)

Webster definitely pushes the boundaries when dealing with such serious themes as murder and torture, but his was a society that made public spectacles out of such incredibly barbaric acts as beheading, burning at the stake and, worst of all, being hanged, drawn and quartered. In our society, the moral perspective is refined and our human rights are respected. If some of the audience laughs during these scenes then, as Liz Shaffer suggests, it may be out of discomfort or it may be because our reality is so different from Webster's that we are fortunate enough to regard the kind of excessive brutality that he depicts as primarily a vicarious cinematic experience rather than as a visceral everyday reality.

Language

Poetic language

In *The Age of Shakespeare* (1908), the eminent author and literary critic Algernon Charles Swinburne defines Webster's greatness as being the product of his sublime use of language. When commenting on the 'many poets in the age of Shakespeare', Swinburne declares that 'Mere literary power, mere poetic beauty … was given – except by exceptional fits and starts – to none of the poets of their time but only to Shakespeare and to Webster.'

Webster's work undoubtedly is intensely poetic and thus resonates with numerous emotive and highly vivid imagery patterns. These are seamlessly woven into the fabric of the play and are, as with all true poetry, expressed in beautifully condensed language, thus enabling them to explode with multiple layers of meaning. A perfect example is when Antonio declares of the Duchess: 'She stains the time past, lights the time to come' (I.1). This image is as beautiful as it is complex. Editors generally read this as suggesting that the metaphorical luminosity of her physical and spiritual essence is so great that she eclipses the past and puts it into shade. The image is even more poetic, however, if read as signifying that she is pure white light, which shines radiantly into the future from the prism of the present and leaves a gorgeous rainbow spectrum of colour in its wake (see the Context box at the bottom of page 60). The Duchess continues to be associated with light throughout the rest of the play. On seeing her strangled body, Ferdinand declares 'Cover her face. Mine eyes dazzle' (IV.2), and in her death scene Webster strongly suggests that she is going to heaven, which, of course, is resplendent in God's glory.

CRITICAL VIEW

Timothy Fox asks, 'is "the skull beneath the skin" the vision of a moralist or a purveyor of horror?' (*A Discussion of Morality and Horror in* The Duchess of Malfi *and* Edward II, 2002).

Build critical skills

Assuming that Webster is 'a moralist' rather than 'a purveyor of horror', Act IV needs very careful staging so that the horror achieves its intended purpose of portraying the terrifying excesses of tyranny. If the audience laughs, then is it a fault with the play, or with the players?

Another facet of Webster's poetry, as L.G. Salingar notes, is that he 'is highly ingenious in the rendering of sensations...' ('Tourneur and the Tragedy of Revenge' in *The Pelican Guide to English Literature, Volume 2*, 1963). Salingar's observation is related to Webster's depiction of physical sensation but it is equally valid for his presentation of emotional experience. This is perfectly exemplified in Act IV scene 2 when the Duchess declares, 'Th'heaven o'er my head seems made of molten brass, / The earth of flaming sulphur...' It is the intense physicality of these images of extreme heat and entrapment that enables Webster so vividly to portray the intensity of her despair.

(For more on Webster's poetry, see Extended commentary 2 on page 88 of this guide.)

Charnel house imagery

One of the more emotive of Webster's imagery patterns, as both George Bernard Shaw and T.S. Eliot note, reverberates with images of death and physical decay. Bosola provides many of the contributions to this motif. As he declares to the Old Lady, 'Though we are eaten up of lice, and worms, / And though continually we bear about us / A rotten and dead body, we delight / To hide it in rich tissue...' (II.1).

This theme is resumed in Bosola's vicious verbal attack on the Duchess after she has been imprisoned by her brothers: 'What's this flesh? A little crudded milk, fantastical puff paste: our bodies are weaker than those paper prisons boys use to keep flies in – more contemptible, since ours is to preserve earth worms' (IV.2). In what seems a dark parody of Shakespeare's famous 'What a piece of work is man!' speech (*Hamlet*, 1603), Webster does not allow Bosola to speculate on the noble and god-like qualities of man so extoled by Hamlet, but only on what Hamlet folornly referred to as 'this quintessence of dust'.

But through 'This talk fit for a charnel' (IV.2), as the Duchess terms it, Webster advances the play's intensely moral dialectic. Firstly, as we are informed by

Antonio at the very outset, corrupt governance creates a corrupt society: **'but if 't chance / Some cursed example poison 't near the head, / Death and diseases through the whole land spread.'** Thus the language of physical decay is emblematic of a society in which moral corruption has become rampant.

Secondly, Webster uses 'charnel talk' to underscore the eternal truth stated in the Bible, that 'Man that is born of a woman is of few days and full of trouble' (Job 14:1). Thus Webster reminds his audience of man's essential mortality and, therefore, advances one of the major themes of the play, the meaninglessness of the ruthless pursuit of self-interest at the expense of one's immortal soul. As A.C. Swinburne triumphantly asserts, 'there is no poet morally nobler than Webster…' (*The Age of Shakespeare*, 1908).

> Top ten quotation

Religious imagery

Politics and theology are closely linked in the moral landscape of the play and Webster reinforces his message through the use of semantic fields that reference the Bible. Thus in Antonio's opening speech, 'a judicious king' who rids himself of the 'flatt'ring sycophants' and other 'dissolute / And infamous persons', and who then replaces these with 'a most provident council' will have created 'a blessed government'. Webster must surely be referring to King James' own court here (see 'Contexts', p. 65).

The devil himself is not seen to be obviously at work within the play (unlike in Christopher Marlowe's *Dr Faustus* or Shakespeare's *Macbeth*). Antonio's opening analysis, though, clearly suggests that a government not run according to the ideal cannot be 'blessed' and, therefore, it must perforce stand vulnerable and defenceless in the face of evil. The malevolent forces in the play, however, are not demons but men who are possessed by evil. Webster has Antonio say of the Cardinal's pronouncements that 'the devil speaks in them' (I.1), and towards the end of the play he has Malateste say of Ferdinand ''Twas nothing but pure kindness in the devil, / To rock his own child' (V.4).

Through the use of yet another devil reference, Webster has Antonio highlight ambition, which is clearly one of the main impetuses to commit evil within the play. When the Duchess offers him her ring as she proposes to him, Antonio, being a virtuous man, immediately questions his own motives regarding such a dramatic rise in status: 'There is a saucy and ambitious devil / Is dancing in this circle' (I.1). Ambition is also what drives Bosola to oversee the brothers' evil and thus Webster similarly taints him, for example when the Duchess asks him 'What devil art thou that counterfeits heaven's thunder?' (III.5).

The Duchess, on the other hand, who rules a well-ordered court with Antonio's aid, is associated with goodliness from beginning to end. In Antonio's initial eulogy of her, he extols her Christian virtue, stating 'her nights, nay more, her very sleeps,

Build critical skills

Is the play primarily 'directed towards chaos' as T.S. Eliot suggests, or is there clear evidence of God's providence as the governing force in human affairs?

Taking it further ▶

For an even-more-direct analysis of the toxic impact of 'vaulting ambition' on both self and society, read Shakespeare's *Macbeth*, Act I scene 7.

/ Are more in heaven than other ladies' shrifts' (I.1). And at her death, Webster has the Duchess ask her executioners to 'pull down heaven upon me' (IV.2).

Aphorisms, parables and sententiae

In line with the Senecan model of tragedy, Webster further deepens the moral profundity of the play through the frequent introduction of wise sayings, which appear as aphorisms, parables and sententiae. Interestingly, he does not reserve these just for the use of characters with unquestionable moral stature.

◥ An **aphorism** is a succinct statement that embodies an astute general truth, for example Castruchio says: 'It is fitting a soldier arise to be a prince, but not necessary a prince descend to be a captain!' (I.1).

◥ A **parable** is a short allegorical story that illustrates a moral or spiritual truth, for example the Duchess' dog-fish story at the end of Act III when countering Bosola's belligerent accusation that Antonio is a 'base, low fellow'.

◥ A **sententia** is very similar to an aphorism in that it is also a succinct saying that imparts a profound moral or philosophical truth. In Elizabethan and Jacobean drama, sententiae often appear at the ends of scenes in rhymed couplets, for example Ferdinand's lines: 'That friend a great man's ruin strongly checks, / Who rails into his belief, all his defects' (III.1).

Prose versus blank verse

Many critics have noted that Webster often uses prose to frame Bosola's speeches, but exactly why he does this is uncertain. It might be to emphasise Bosola's lower status in society; or, as the other major characters generally speak in blank verse, it might be to set Bosola apart and so add a distinctive voice to his role as a satirical and extremely cynical commentator on events; or it might be because much of what he says was considered too coarse or too brutal for verse:

> He and his brother are like plum trees that grow crooked over standing pools: they are rich, and o'erladen with fruit, but none but crows, pies, and caterpillars feed on them. Could I be one of their flatt'ring panders, I would hang on their ears like a horse-leech till I were full, and then drop off.

(I.1)

Bosola's cynicism arises from the fact that he longs to be a beneficiary of the corruption that he affects to disdain. Bosola's prose, however, is far from prosaic because of Webster's rich use of metaphorical language. The image of the unhealthy stagnant pool beautifully contrasts with the free-flowing fountain simile through which Antonio characterises a well-run court at the beginning

---

Build critical skills

In your view, does the fact that Webster shares sententious wisdom with good and evil characters alike suggest insincerity on his part and thus undermine the credibility of the moral fabric of the play?

of the play, and the animal imagery conjures up a powerful impression of a debased humanity. It should be remembered, though, that Webster does not confine the use of prose solely to Bosola and that Bosola also uses blank verse as well as occasional rhyming couplets.

Blank verse, which forms the majority of the dialogue, is verse that does not rhyme. It often has a definite metre, usually of iambic pentameter. Iambic pentameter is a pattern of five metric feet in which each metric foot consists of one short/unstressed syllable followed by one long/stressed syllable. It sounds rather like 'de dum, de dum, de dum, de dum, de dum'. In the example below, the first three lines are written in blank verse, but note the transition to a rhyming heroic couplet in order to emphasise the idea that is the play's main argument:

> Consid'ring duly that a prince's court
> Is like a common fountain, whence should flow
> Pure silver drops in general, but if 't chance
> Some cursed example poison 't near the head,
> Death and diseases through the whole land spread.

(I.1)

In the above speech, the line lengths are regular as each one can be read so that there are exactly ten syllables, for example by shortening 'considering' to 'consid'ring' (as it has been spelt in the above quotation) and 'general' to 'gen'ral'. The final line, however, is a subtle departure from iambic pentameter as 'Death' is a heavily stressed syllable, and this unexpected break in the pattern enables the actor's delivery of the word to be even more emphatic.

It is the case, however, that much of the blank verse in the play is irregular and so cannot be made to conform to ten syllables per line. Passages of blank verse frequently consist of lines of clearly differing lengths, have irregular stresses and make great use of **enjambment** and **caesura**. Thus the boundary between blank verse and prose is often blurred. This has the effect of making the dialogue sound more conversational and naturalistic, thus enabling Webster to imbue his chilling tale with a shocking sense of realism. By the Jacobean period, Shakespeare and the other major dramatists of the age all used blank verse in this way.

Taking it further ▶

In order to appreciate how much more fluid and natural the use of blank verse had become by the Jacobean period, read the first few pages of Christopher Marlowe's *Tamburlaine the Great* (1587), in which the use of blank verse is absolutely regular but also sounds rather artificial.

◁ Top ten quotation

Enjambment: The continuation of a phrase or a clause beyond the end of a line of verse as opposed to end-stopping (concluding) the idea at the end of a line. Enjambment generally results in a medial caesura.

Caesura: A naturally occurring pause in a line of verse. A medial caesura falls in the middle of a line.

Target your thinking

- How can setting *The Duchess of Malfi* within a broad range of contexts deepen your understanding of the play and the ways in which different audiences might respond to it? (**AO3**)
- What links might be traced between *The Duchess of Malfi* and various other literary texts? (**AO4**)
- What different critical positions might be applied to *The Duchess of Malfi* to extend your knowledge of the text? (**AO1**)
- How can applying various critical approaches enrich your understanding of *The Duchess of Malfi* and the ways in which different readers might interpret it? (**AO5**)

Webster's life and works

Little is known for certain about John Webster's life, but it is a fact that he was born in London between 1578 and 1580. His father was a prosperous coach-maker and a prominent member of the Guild of Merchant Taylors, one of the most prestigious craft guilds. Given the strictly hierarchical nature of Jacobean society, however, he could still be looked down on by the more socially elevated. In 1617, some three or four years after *The Duchess of Malfi* was first performed, Webster was lampooned in a poem by Henry Fitzgeffrey as 'crabbed Websterio / The playwright–cartwright'. The word 'crabbed' might well be an attempt to undermine Webster's various stabs at the unfairness of the power balance in his society by characterising them as nothing more than bad temper, but the slur on his family background is self-evident.

Details of Webster's education are sketchy, but it is speculated that owing to his father's position, he may well have attended the Merchant Taylors' school, where he would have received a Classical education. It is also speculated that he began training as a lawyer in 1598 in the Inns of Court. By 1602, Webster had begun work as a dramatist. Webster's date of death is generally recorded as 1634.

Webster's major tragedies

Webster's career reached its height between 1612 and 1616, though *The White Devil*, the first of his great tragedies, was initially unsuccessful. It was premiered by the Queen's Men at the Red Bull Theatre in Clerkenwell, north London, during the winter season at the beginning of 1612. Webster complained that: 'most of the people that come to that playhouse, resemble those ignorant asses…' Webster was more fortunate with *The Duchess of Malfi*, which was performed roughly two years later by a rival troupe, the King's Men. Initially, they presented it at the indoor Blackfriars, performing to a more courtly and educated private audience, and in the summer they transferred it to the Globe, their open-air auditorium where they performed to a socially varied audience.

King James' court

Webster uses the convenient distance of history and an Italian setting to explore some of the 'hot' social and political issues of his day. Antonio's opening description of a 'judicious' king very much reflects the tenor of James' own treatise on good kingship, as set out in *Basilikon Doron* (1599), the title meaning 'Royal Gift'. The book was written for his eldest son and heir, Prince Henry, who never had the opportunity to succeed to the throne owing to his premature death in 1612. In the book, James advises Prince Henry to choose his courtiers and advisors with great care, exhorting him to 'Make your Court and company to be a pattern of godliness and all honest virtues to all the rest of the people.' James also instructs Henry on the difference between 'a lawful good king and an usurping tyrant'. He explains that 'The one acknowledgeth himself ordained for his people having received from God a burthen of government whereof he must be accountable: The other thinketh his people ordained for him, a pray to his appetites…'

▲ King James, by John de Critz the Elder

Despite his various disagreements with the English Parliament over what they deemed his improvident spending, James reaffirmed his commitment to being a law-abiding king in a speech to Parliament in 1610: 'And therefore a king governing in a settled kingdom leaves to be a king and degenerates into a tyrant as soon as he leaves off to rule according to his laws.' Webster, having begun his play with a description that perfectly accords with James' definition of a well-run court and a 'lawful king' as described in *Basilikon Doron*, then appears to explore the impact of James' definition of a tyrant via the Cardinal and Ferdinand. They do indeed abuse their power in order to satisfy their 'appetites'. The Cardinal makes Julia 'a pray' to his sexual desire and then destroys her when he has tired of her. Ferdinand's 'appetite' is directed towards his sister and Webster actually has him express the desire to drink her blood after he hears Bosola's report that she has just given birth. Ferdinand is also described by Delio as a 'spider' who uses the law 'To entangle those shall feed him' (I.1). And just as she is about to be strangled, the Duchess declares 'Go tell my brothers when I am laid out, / They then may feed in quiet' (IV.2).

Although James himself may not have been a tyrant, the problem with his idealisation of the role of a king was that the running of his court fell far short of the model that he had proposed. James had a well-known penchant for his 'favourites', these initially being young men that he had brought down from Scotland with him. These favourites were able to inveigle themselves with James through their good looks and by pandering to his ego and, for this

Context

John Marston's 1604 play *Parasitaster, or The Fawn*, is also regarded as an attack on the moral impropriety, flattery and general misconduct in King James' court.

▲ Robert Carr, Earl of Somerset, by John Hoskins

questionable service, they were handsomely rewarded. One of the methods by which James funded this profligate spending, and which caused so much friction between himself and Parliament, was to sell off government offices and honourable titles such as peerages and knighthoods. This had the double effect of debasing the value of a title and filling key government positions with men who lacked talent and integrity.

Antonio's opening speech seems to articulate concerns about this behaviour when advocating the example of the 'French court':

> In seeking to reduce both state and people
> To a fixed order, their judicious king
> Begins at home, quits first his royal palace
> Of flatt'ring sycophants, of dissolute
> And infamous persons...

(I.1)

In *Divine Catastrophe of the Kingly Family of the House of Stuarts*, Sir Edward Peyton (1587–1652) describes King James 'as governing by young counsellors, who had not vertue, but vanity ... these nobles being addicted more to pleasure and delights then the school of prudence and wisdome; looking more at their own interest then the common good or piety of life, gave so vast a liberty to their lives, as made an abordment of looseness in many insomuch that strictness of life (which our Saviour requires) was imputed a disgrace; and the vainest counted the wisest...'

At the time when *The Duchess of Malfi* was first performed, the favourite with the most influence over James was Robert Carr. James is reputed to have fallen in love with the seventeen-year-old page in 1607, after the latter was injured during a tilting contest. Solely on the basis of this attraction, Carr rose through the ranks to dizzying heights to become the Earl of Somerset in 1613 and Lord Chamberlain in 1614, making him the single most important official in the King's household.

Context

'...so the love the king showed was as amorously conveyed, as if he had mistaken their sex, and thought them ladies; which I have seen Somerset and Buckingham labour to resemble, in the effeminateness of their dressings...' (Francis Osborne (1593-1659), *Traditional Memoirs of the Reigns of Queen Elizabeth and King James I*).

Ironically, Carr's crash from favour was even more rapid and spectacular than his rise had been. He had become romantically involved with a married aristocrat, Frances Howard, who wished to be free of her husband, Robert Devereaux, the Earl of Essex. Carr's close friend and ally Sir Thomas Overbury had initially supported the liaison, even writing love letters on Carr's behalf, but when the affair became more serious Overbury strenuously opposed Carr's intention to marry Frances. His objection to this was twofold: firstly, Frances was in his view 'noted for her injury and immodesty'; secondly, the Howards were one of the leading Catholic families in the land and Overbury feared that the union with Carr would enable them to gain too much political influence.

In order to assist Carr, James offered Overbury the Russian ambassadorship so as to remove him from court. When Overbury refused, James had him imprisoned in the Tower of London for contempt in April 1613. James then used his influence to force through the annulment of Frances' existing marriage on the basis of the union never having been consummated owing to Devereux's alleged impotency. To sustain the charge, Frances had to submit to an intimate internal medical examination so as to demonstrate that she was still a virgin. As she had insisted on being veiled during the examination, however, it was widely rumoured that the virgin examined was not Frances but a substitute, as is indicated by a popular verse of the time, 'This dame was inspected but fraud interjected…' The annulment was granted in September 1613 and James' blatantly partisan misuse of his power was widely noted. Carr and Frances wed in the December in spectacular style. Sir Thomas Overbury, on the other hand, unexpectedly died in September 1613 while still in the Tower.

Meanwhile, Carr's enemies at court worked hard throughout the latter part of 1614 to supplant his influence with James by trying to interest the King in a new favourite, a handsome young man named George Villiers (later to become the Duke of Buckingham). Fortunately for them, in 1615 evidence suddenly came to light that Overbury's death had in fact been orchestrated by a vengeful Frances. She had arranged for him to be poisoned and Carr, rather than protect his friend (as he had promised), may well have been complicit in the crime. Frances eventually confessed, though Carr continued to deny any culpability. Both were found guilty in 1616 and sentenced to death, but their sentences were commuted and they were imprisoned in the Tower, from where they were released in 1621. They were fully pardoned by James in 1624 but never returned to court, living out the rest of their lives in relative obscurity.

Taking it further ▷

To find out more about the corruption of James's court and the death of Sir Thomas Overbury, you might like to read Anne Somerset's 2004 study 'Unnatural Murder: Poison In The Court Of James I'.

The Duchess of Malfi was first performed in 1614 and thus premiered after the debacle of the annulment but before the uproar over Overbury's murder — although the 1623 published version of the text may well reflect Webster's awareness of both events. It is clear, however, that Webster's evocation of a court riven by favouritism, factionalism, betrayal and intrigue aptly captures the political realities of the day. Thus, the extent to which James' government fell

▲ Frances Howard, Countess of Somerset

Context

Overbury, a well-known poet and essayist, was an associate of Webster's and so Webster would have taken a keen interest in the affair.

Context

'The court is factious grown through the desire / That everyone hath gotten to aspire' (George Withers, *Of Ambition*, 1613).

Great Chain of Being: the idea that every thing in the universe had its 'place' in a divinely planned hierarchical order, which was pictured as a vertically extended chain.

short of the King's own ideal as set out in *Basilikon Doron,* and in the 'French court' as described by Antonio in his opening speech, is of central importance. Webster is clearly mirroring his audience's unfavourable perception of James' court when he has Bosola describe the Aragonian brothers as 'plum trees that grow crooked over standing pools: they are rich, and o'erladen with fruit, but none but crows, pies, and caterpillars feed on them' (l.1).

Context

Anne Turner, a confidante of Frances Howard who was hanged as an accomplice in the murder of Sir Thomas Overbury, stated at her trial in 1615: 'God bless the King and send him better servants about him, for there is no religion in the most of them, but malice, pride, whoredom, swearing, and rejoicing in the fall of others.'

The political views of Niccolo Machiavelli

In 1513, Niccolò Machiavelli wrote an instructional manual for effective leadership entitled *The Prince*. Despite containing much practical wisdom, the book was widely regarded as advocating evil practices and so was put on the Papacy's List of Banned Books in 1559. Machiavelli's name became synonymous with intrigue and the use of unethical means to acquire or maintain power. A 'machiavel' thus came to mean the type of person who seeks to deceive and manipulate others for personal gain, as in 'Never attempt to win by force what can be won by deception.' Webster's use of this stereotype may well be designed to reflect the scheming, intriguing and general jockeying for position within James' court, but equally it may be a more fundamental reflection on human nature in general as, in truth, it would be difficult to find any society at any point in human history in which at least some of the people at the top behaved in any other way.

Social mobility

As Webster's play powerfully portrays, social mobility was regarded as a threat to the established order. At the top of the Jacobean hierarchy was the king, followed by the aristocracy, which consisted of wealthy nobles who owned great tracts of land and who had a great deal of political sway, though not as much as the king. Below the nobles were the gentry who also owned land and wealth, though considerably less than the nobility. Below the gentry were the middle classes, who included yeoman farmers, merchants and craftsmen. Webster clearly comes from the latter as his father was a prosperous coach-maker. As a manager of the Duchess' household and estates, Antonio also belongs to this class. The general belief in the '**Great Chain of Being**' dictated that class divisions were sacrosanct as the social order had been fixed by God, with the king being placed firmly at the top. Consequently, it was considered unacceptable to marry too far above or below your social standing.

Edward Grimestone's translation of Simon Goulart's *Admirable and Memorable Histories of Our Time* (1607) was another minor source for Webster's play. In it, Grimestone, like Painter before him, condemns Antonio's presumption in marrying above his station, referring to him as a 'Gentleman, who drunke with his owne conceite, and forgetting the respect which hee ought vnto his Ladye and to her house, neither yet remembring his owne meane estate...'

The gap in status between the Duchess and Antonio is particularly wide, as is emphasised by Bosola's demeaning references to 'this base, low fellow' and 'One of no birth' (III.5). People were expected to know their place and to remain there. To do otherwise was regarded as risking social stability and thus threatening to plunge society into chaos and anarchy, exactly as we see happen in Webster's play. Of course, the chaos and anarchy depicted in the world of Malfi can equally be viewed as resulting from the behaviour of the small selfish political elite whose grip on power is both paranoid and relentless.

Women in society

Despite the towering example Queen Elizabeth had set, Jacobean society remained firmly patriarchal and in many respects misogynistic, as is indicated by Joseph Swetnam's infamous pamphlet, *The Arraignment of Lewd, Idle, Froward, and Unconstant Women* (1615), in which he makes such adversarial declarations as that 'women are all necessary evils...' Misogyny was by no means universal, however, and Swetnam's tract also received condemnation. In *A Mouzell for Melastomus* (1617), a direct response to what she terms the 'Foule-mouthed Barker', Rachel Speght asserts that God 'created woman to bee a solace vnto him [man], to participate of his sorrowes, partake of his pleasures, and as a good yokefellow beare part of his burthen.'

Legally, women's choices were almost entirely circumscribed by their fathers, or by their brothers if a father had died, and then by their husbands. The only exception was a widow, who after the death of her husband was freed from the disempowering legal concept of coverture and so became responsible for herself and her own property. It was perfectly possible for a widow to remarry, although this was frowned on by some. In William Painter's version of the story, the Duchess' death is justified via his condemnation of her for her lust, her social impropriety, her disobedience to her brothers and her impious behaviour in respect of the feigned pilgrimage. Webster's reimagining, however, is far more sympathetic to the Duchess' rights as a widow.

Context

Thomas Archer helped fuel this fierce debate about the nature of women, publishing both Swetnam's and Speght's pamphlets as well as the 1623 edition of Webster's plays.

TASK

Write a brief summary of the ways in which the Duchess and Antonio's relationship matches Speght's description of companionate marriage.

Context

In his character sketch *A Virtuous Widow*, Sir Thomas Overbury suggests that a moral widow will not remarry; in *An Ordinary Widow*, he declares 'he that hath her is lord but of a filthy purchase...'

Context

Edward Grimestone also frowns upon the Duchess' behaviour in his very short 1607 version of the story, referring to the Duchess' 'lascivious eye', her defiance of the 'good advice of her Bretheren, and honorable Kinsfolkes', and her wilfulness in marrying beneath her social position.

Admittedly, some of Webster's male characters do exhibit typical contemporary attitudes to women, for example Bosola's misogynistic comments addressed to the Old Lady, and the Cardinal's to Julia. Webster's play challenges such attitudes, however, by investing the Duchess with a moving, tragic courage and dignity despite the very human faults that she displays. Rather than condemn her, Webster appears to condemn the oppressive society that initially constrains and then ultimately destroys her.

Professor Sara Jayne Steen has suggested that Webster may well have had in mind the example of Lady Arabella Stuart (1575–1615), the first cousin of King James, when creating his version of the Duchess. In 1610, Arabella had secretly married William Seymour, a fellow aristocrat, without James' permission. James had the couple separately imprisoned but they managed to remain in communication and so formed a plan to escape. James thwarted their attempt to elope to France, however, and had Arabella imprisoned in the Tower where she died in 1615 of illness exacerbated by despair and malnutrition. Arabella's tragic outcome certainly exemplifies the precarious position that even high-born women occupied in Jacobean society.

Decadence, disease and death

Jacobeans lived in close proximity to disease, violence and death, and thus it is no wonder that morbidity is such a powerful theme in the play. Infant mortality was high and most people were lucky to survive beyond their thirties. In particular, frequent outbreaks of the plague (Black Death) devastated the population. Symptoms included: high fever; painful swelling in the armpits, legs, neck or groin; delirium; muscular pain; and bleeding in the lungs, which would lead to coughing up blood.

Although there was an awareness of the role of poor sanitation in causing illness, there was also a lingering belief that such outbreaks were a result of God punishing man for his sinfulness. Thomas Dekker, a popular pamphleteer and playwright of the day who collaborated with Webster on the writing of two plays during 1604–06, joyfully declared in *The Wonderfull Yeare* (1603):

> *God stuck valiantlie to us, For behold, up rises a comfortable Sun out of the north, whose glorious beames (like a fan) dispersed all thick and contagious clowdes.*

Dekker is alluding to James' ascendency to the throne as a result of Queen Elizabeth I having died in March of that year, and he is clearly expressing the hope that the new King's rule will receive God's blessing, thus freeing the nation from the scourge of plague. Unfortunately, 1603–04 saw an exceptionally severe outbreak, which killed around a fifth of London's population and closed the theatres for the best part of a year. Plague remained a constant threat throughout, and indeed beyond, James' reign. Thus, when Antonio declares, **'but if 't chance / Some cursed example poison 't near the head, / Death and diseases through the whole land spread'** (I.1), the meaning may well be

▲ Portrait of Arabella Stuart (1575–1615), cousin of King James I of England and daughter of Charles Stuart

Top ten quotation

as much literal as metaphorical, as Webster is possibly articulating a common concern that the corruption in James' court could lead to further pestilence.

Religion

Apart from a brief return to Catholicism under Mary I, England had been a Protestant country since Henry VIII's break with the Roman Catholic Church in the 1530s. Catholics were presented as ritualistic idol-worshippers who were politically and morally corrupt. Anti-Catholic prejudice was enshrined in the law, with harsh punishments for refusing to follow Protestant doctrine. England had also been at war with Catholic states such as Spain, whose armada had been triumphantly defeated in 1588, while Catholic conspiracies such as the 1605 Gunpowder Plot reinforced suspicion of those who espoused the forbidden faith.

The Thirty Years' War broke out and engulfed much of Europe during the years 1618–48. This was the result of the future Holy Roman Emperor Ferdinand II, in his position as King of Bohemia, trying to impose Roman Catholicism upon the territories over which he ruled. Although *The Duchess of Malfi* was first performed in 1614, it was not published until 1623 and thus Malateste's reference to the Emperor preparing for war at the beginning of Act III scene 3 may well be mirroring the international political and religious tensions of the age. One way to understand the magnitude of this seventeenth century conflict might be to think of the political and theological divide between Protestants and Catholics as analogous to the political and ideological divide between capitalism and communism in the twentieth century. The latter divide, which we term the Cold War, put the world on the brink of nuclear Armageddon on a number of occasions post-World War II.

Jacobean dramatists who wanted to attack religious or political corruption and hypocrisy at home therefore had a convenient scapegoat in European Catholicism, and Italian and Spanish settings were particularly useful for exploiting the suspicion with, and contempt in which, foreign countries were held. Jacobean tragedy teems with Machiavellian cardinals and corrupt Popes. In 1618 the Venetian envoy Orazio Busino claimed that the English 'never put on any public show whatever, be it tragedy or satire or comedy, into which they do not insert some Catholic churchman's vices and wickednesses, making mock and scorn of him'. Referring to the role of the Cardinal in *The Duchess of Malfi*, he concluded that 'all this was acted in condemnation of the grandeur of the church, which they despise and which in this kingdom they hate to the death'. Despite the anti-Catholic prejudice in Jacobean society, however, Webster and his audience would have been only too aware that clerical corruption was not confined to the Catholic faith.

Critical contexts

AO5 requires you to demonstrate that you understand the meaning of a text is not 'fixed', and thus in the examination you may be required to consider other readers' or critics' interpretations while you are in the process of writing your

▲ Pope Paul V Borghese (Pope 1605–21), by Caravaggio

CRITICAL VIEW

G.K. Hunter has defined the use of an Italian setting in Jacobean drama 'as a mode of human experience rather than as a country' ('English Folly and Italian Vice', in *Dramatic Identities and Cultural Tradition: Studies in Shakespeare and His Contemporaries*, 1978). Hunter is pointing out that although ostensibly set in another country, Jacobean dramas were quintessentially analyses of life in Jacobean England.

own response to the question. With a long-established classic such as *The Duchess of Malfi*, a great many interpretations have arisen over the course of time. Your acknowledgement of some of the more significant of these may be supported by reference to the ideas of named critics, or to particular critical perspectives. As you do this, try to distinguish between critical readings that reflect the preoccupations of the age in which the critics lived, and critical readings that are more directly related to the intellectual and cultural background of the Jacobean period. Of course, both may be equally valid and impart crucial insights because the common denominator at the heart of Webster's play, like that of most great literature, is the search for meaning (or lack thereof) in human existence.

Ultimately, you will need to arrive at a valid personal interpretation of the play through an understanding of the various critical approaches. Critics often take diametrically opposed stances on the aesthetic integrity and/or moral worth of Webster's work. Love him or loathe him, Webster continues to arouse a passionate debate!

It is worth, noting, however, that there is the potential for criticism to be written partly as a means of self-promotion for the critic. Thus it can deteriorate into verbal sparring, which might not be as sincere as it could be. 'Ripping somebody's reputation is recognized blood sport,' says Clive James in his article 'Whither the Hatchet Job?' (*New York Times*, June 2013). Ian Jack's intensely hostile critique, *The Case of John Webster* (1949), seems as much targeted at fellow eminent critic E.M.W. Tillyard as it does at Webster himself: 'When Dr Tillyard goes on to say that Webster's characters belong "to a world of violent crime and violent change, of sin, blood and repentance, yet to a world loyal to a theological scheme" … he is … uttering a dangerous half-truth.' Jack disputes that Webster has a genuinely Christian worldview – and seems as keen on debunking his fellow critic, Tillyard, as he does Webster!

Performance criticism

Performance criticism differs from other genres of literary criticism because instead of considering the play as a text, it considers it in terms of how meaning is created through the medium of the performance. There is the issue, however, that a text may be appropriated to create new meanings that are primarily relevant to contemporary society, thus illustrating textual instability.

There are actually some surviving testimonials from 1623 by Webster's contemporaries, although whether they relate more to the newly published play as a text rather than to the play as a performance is unclear. Thomas Middleton (1580–1627) describes it as a 'masterpiece of tragedy' and John Ford (1586–1639), another famous playwright of the period, correctly forecast that it would bring Webster 'A lasting fame'.

Recent reviews of Dominic Dromgoole's 2014 production of the play staged at the Sam Wanamaker Playhouse, Shakespeare's Globe, and starring Gemma

Arterton in the lead role, would suggest that four hundred years later the play remains essential, relevant and acclaimed. Liz Schafer, writing for the *Times Higher Education* website, describes it as 'a convincingly chilling tale of sororicide' and notes that 'Act 4 is dedicated to displaying the psychological torture of a woman by totalitarian despots.' Michael Billington, writing for the *Guardian*, describes the part of the Duchess as 'one of the great female roles in the canon' and, taking a nihilistic philosophical stance, asserts, 'If the play continues to attract us, I suspect it is because we instinctively recognise the Websterian view of life as "a general mist of error" without sense or purpose while also responding to the image of endurance and fortitude symbolised by the Duchess herself.' Charles Spencer, writing for *The Telegraph*, is more focused on the 'chilling thrills and dark poetry of this cruel, unsettling drama'.

Whether it be because of its potential for politicising the continuing patriarchal mistreatment of women in certain cultures, or because of its abiding philosophical poignancy or, at a purely aesthetic level, because of the exciting plot and sheer magnificence of Webster's poetry, the play has certainly stood the test of time.

Below are some of the more relevant critical perspectives that have been reflected in the margin boxes throughout this guide.

Critical viewpoints

Marxist criticism

Based on the ideas of political philosopher Karl Marx (1818–83), this critical viewpoint explores texts in terms of the historical circumstances in which they were written, with an emphasis on the interactions between the social classes. Thus Ferdinand's and the Cardinal's objections to Antonio can be viewed as an aristocratic aversion to an emerging bourgeoisie. A Marxist perspective might also express some sympathy for Bosola's justification that he had acted 'Much 'gainst mine own good nature, yet i'th'end / Neglected' (V.5). Indeed, as modern sociology informs us, inequality and limited opportunity breed a resentment that often manifests itself in extreme antisocial behaviour.

New Historicism

First developed in the 1980s, this approach explores texts in terms of how they both were influenced by and are reflective of their cultural milieu (the intellectual, political and social context in which they were written). It explores literature alongside other contemporaneous cultural texts, including such non-literary texts as pamphlets and sermons. This is very much the spirit in which this guide has been composed and so should enable you to address AO3, 'Demonstrate understanding of the significance and influence of the contexts in which literary texts are written and received.'

▲ Gemma Arterton as the Duchess in Dominic Dromgoole's 2014 production

Taking it further ▶

On the BBC website, there are some excerpts from this performance. Search for 'BBC: *A Tragedy by Candlelight*'.

73

CRITICAL VIEW

'*The Duchess of Malfi* stands as a perfect fable of emergent liberalism. The text valorises women's equality to the point where the Duchess woos Antonio, repudiating the hierarchy of birth in favour of individual virtue…' (Catherine Belsey, *The Subject of Tragedy: Identity and Difference in Renaissance Drama*, 1985).

Feminist criticism

This viewpoint might give rise to an interpretation of the play as being about gender stereotyping. Whether Webster's play exhibits feminist sympathies, or whether on the contrary it accepts and endorses the patriarchal rule and misogyny of his time, is open to debate. A consideration of the issue, however, can only enhance our exploration of the characters of the Duchess, Julia and Cariola. Many modern audiences might see Webster as a staunch feminist who empathises with the Duchess' plight in not being allowed to 'choose' her own 'mate', and might cite his ultimate condemnation of the cruelty and hypocrisy of her brothers in order to uphold this interpretation. Julia embraces her sexuality in a confident and abandoned way and refuses to conform to male stereotypes. Instead she pursues her own path and dies faithful to the way in which she lived. This renders her a very sympathetic character to modern female theatre-goers, who are arguably still living in a society entrenched in the virgin/ whore dichotomy.

Equally, though, an alternative feminist reading might be that the play actually upholds Jacobean male perspectives, in that all three female characters die as a result of their attempts to evade or subvert male order. The final scene of the play is dominated by male characters and even the remaining heir of the Duchess' love match, though 'hopeful' in his possible inheritance of his 'mother's right', has been given a horoscope predicting a premature and violent death. Perhaps, then, Webster suggests that women will never be able successfully to challenge and overcome male rule in such a patriarchal society. (For more on this, see the Women in society section of the 'Contexts' chapter, p. 69.)

Psychoanalytic criticism

Much psychoanalytic criticism is based on the theories of Sigmund Freud (1856–1939) and explores the effect of repressed subconscious desires on behaviour. A perfectly plausible Freudian reading of the play might focus on the nature of Ferdinand's obsession with his sister's sexuality. It might suggest that his overwhelming fury at her rejection of the chastity that he tries to enforce upon her arises out of a forbidden sexual yearning that he himself can never fulfil. If he can't have her, nobody else can either!

Assessment Objectives and skills

As you consider the Assessment Objectives, think about the precise demands of your particular examination board. For example, all AOs are tested in questions set for *The Duchess of Malfi* by WJEC Eduqas, but those set by OCR do not test AO2 and those set by Edexcel do not test AO4 or AO5. The play could be used as AQA A NEA (coursework) too.

> **AO1** Articulate informed, personal and creative responses to literary texts, using associated concepts and terminology, and coherent, accurate written expression.

To do well with AO1 you need to write fluently, structuring your essay carefully, guiding your reader clearly through your line of argument and using the sophisticated vocabulary, including critical terminology, appropriate to an A-level essay. You will need to use frequent embedded quotations to show detailed knowledge of, and demonstrate familiarity with, the whole text. Your aim is to produce a well written academic essay employing appropriate discourse markers (connectives that aid the flow of an argument) in order to create a coherently shaped response.

> **AO2** Analyse ways in which meanings are shaped in literary texts.

This AO is not applicable to the OCR question on *The Duchess of Malfi*.

Strong students do not work only on a lexical level, but also write well on the generic and structural elements of the text, so it is useful to start by analysing those larger elements before considering Webster's language. To discuss language in detail you will need to quote from the play, analyse that quotation and use it to illuminate your argument. Moreover, since you will at times need to make points about larger generic and organisational features of the text that are much too long to quote in full, being able to reference effectively is just as important as mastering the art of the embedded quotation. Practise writing in analytical sentences, comprising a brief quotation or close reference, a definition or description of the feature you intend to analyse, an explanation of how this feature has been used, and an evaluation of its effectiveness.

> **AO3** Demonstrate understanding of the significance and influence of the contexts in which literary texts are written and received.

To access AO3 you need to think about how the contexts of production and reception can affect texts, as well as about other contextual factors, including literature, culture, biography, geography, society, history, genre and intertextuality. Place the play at the heart of the web of contextual factors that you feel have had the most impact upon it. Examiners want to see a sense of contextual alertness woven seamlessly into the fabric of your essay rather than a clumsily bolted-on website rehash or some recycled history notes. Show you understand that literary works contain encoded representations of the cultural, moral, religious, racial and political values of the society from which they emerged, and that over time attitudes and ideas change until the views they reflect may no longer be widely shared.

AO4   Explore connections across literary texts.

This AO is not applicable to the Edexcel question on *The Duchess of Malfi*.

If your examination board requires you to compare and contrast one or more other texts with *The Duchess of Malfi*, you must try to find specific points of comparison, rather than merely generalising. You will find it easier to make connections between texts (of any kind) if you try to balance them as you write. Remember also that connections are not only about finding similarities – differences are just as interesting. Above all, consider how the comparison illuminates each text. Some connections will be thematic, others generic or stylistic.

AO5   Explore literary texts informed by different interpretations.

This AO is not applicable to the Edexcel question on *The Duchess of Malfi*.

For this AO, you should refer to the opinions of critics and remain alert to aspects of the play that are open to interpretation. Your job is to measure your own interpretation of the text against those of other readers. As a text that has generated widely differing responses, *The Duchess of Malfi* lends itself readily to the range of interpretations (see Critical contexts in the 'Contexts' chapter, p. 71, and elsewhere in this guide). Try to convey an awareness of multiple readings as well as an understanding that, as the critic Roland Barthes suggested, a text's meaning is dependent as much upon what you bring to it as what the author left there. Using modal verb phrases – such as *may be seen as…*, *might be interpreted as…* or *could represent…* – shows you know that different readers will interpret texts in different ways at different times. The key word here is plurality; there is no single meaning or one right answer. Relish getting your teeth into the views of published critics to push forward your own argument, but always keep in mind that meanings in texts are shifting and unstable rather than fixed and permanent.

Summary

Overall, the hallmarks of a successful A-level essay that hits all five AOs include:

- A clear introduction that orientates the reader and outlines your main argument.
- A coherent and conceptualised argument that relates to the question title.
- Confident movement around the text rather than a relentless chronological trawl through it.
- Apt and effective quotations or references adapted to make sense within the context of your own sentences.
- A range of effective points about the writer's dramatic methods.
- A strong and personally engaged awareness of how a text can be interpreted by different readers and audiences in different ways at different times.
- A sense that you are prepared to take on a good range of critical and theoretical perspectives.
- A conclusion that effectively summarises and consolidates your response and relates it back to your essay title.

Building skills 1: Structuring your writing

This section focuses on organising your written responses to convey your ideas as clearly and effectively as possible: the 'how' of your writing as opposed to the 'what'. More often than not, if your knowledge and understanding of *The Duchess of Malfi* is sound, a disappointing mark or grade will be down to one of two common mistakes: misreading the question or failing to organise your response economically and effectively. In an examination you'll be lucky if you can demonstrate 5 per cent of what you know about the play; however, if it's the right 5 per cent, that's all you need to gain full marks.

Understanding your examination

It's important to prepare for the specific type of response your examination body sets with regard to *The Duchess of Malfi*: if you are being examined by Edexcel, it will be Open Book; for Eduqas and for OCR, Closed Book. For Open Book, you will have a clean copy of the text available to you in the exam, but it must be an edition that does not include paraphrases or translations of the original text, or critical essays or study notes; for Closed Book, you won't be allowed to take a copy of the text into the examination.

In an Open Book exam, there can be no possible excuse for failing to quote relevantly, regularly and accurately. To gain a high mark, you are expected to focus in detail on specific passages. In a Closed Book exam, because the examiners are well aware that you do not have your text in front of you, their expectations will be different. While you are still expected to support your argument with relevant quotations, close textual references are also encouraged and rewarded. Since you will have had to memorise quotations, slight inaccuracies will not be severely punished. Rather than a forensically detailed analysis of a specific section of *The Duchess of Malfi*, the examiner will expect you to range more broadly across the play to structure your response.

Planning and beginning: locate the debate

Edexcel's A-level sample assessment materials suggest that the examination question they will present you with will require you to explore character or theme or, possibly, an aspect of style. Edexcel's AS paper and A level papers for Eduqas and OCR, on the other hand, are more likely to provide you with a question that invites you to open up a debate about character, theme or style by initially considering a quoted opinion. Although the Edexcel A-level question does not launch you into debate, you should still attempt to think around the main issue or theme in the question and to approach it from a variety of angles.

When answering a debate-type question, the one thing you can be sure of is that exam questions never offer a view that makes no sense at all, or one so blindingly obvious that all anyone can do is agree with it; there will always be a genuine interpretation at stake. To orientate the reader, your introduction needs to address the terms of this debate and to sketch out the outline of how you intend to move the argument forward. Since it's obviously going to be helpful if you actually know this before you start writing, you really do need to plan before you begin to write.

Undertaking a lively debate about some of the ways in which *The Duchess of Malfi* has been and can be interpreted is the DNA of your essay. Of course, any good argument needs to be honest, but to begin by writing 'Yes, I totally agree with this obviously true statement' suggests a fundamental misunderstanding of what studying literature is all about. Any stated view in an examination question is designed to open up critical conversations, not to shut them down.

Student A

This first extract is from a student response to the following Edexcel A-level exam-style question:

Explore the presentation of fate in *The Duchess of Malfi*. You must relate your discussion to relevant contextual factors.

One of Webster's most famous lines occurs just after Bosola has mistakenly murdered Antonio in Act V scene 4, when the malcontent declares 'We are merely the stars' tennis balls, struck and banded / Which way please them'. The metaphor clearly suggests that the attempt to control your own destiny is doomed in the face of a universe that seems determined to frustrate mankind at every point. It is interesting that such a superstitious attitude appears so often, when Jacobean society was fundamentally Christian. This is evidenced by the fact that King James commissioned a new version of the Bible and wrote books on demonology and witchcraft. Webster's play clearly reflects the complicated belief system of the age because as well as the workings of fate he also presents divine providence.

Examiner's commentary

This student:

- immediately addresses the essay question via a most pertinent quotation (**AO1**)
- demonstrates an impressive textual knowledge (**AO2**)
- uses pertinent subject terminology, e.g. 'malcontent' and 'metaphor' (**AO1**)
- correctly and succinctly elucidates the concept of fate as it appears in the drama of the age (**AO3**)
- makes a most relevant and extremely perceptive comment about the seeming contradiction between superstition and religion (**AO3**)
- has excellent SPaG and expression (**AO1**).

In the rest of the essay, the student fully addresses AOs 1–3 (AOs 4 and 5 are not examined by Edexcel for *The Duchess of Malfi*), exploring the theme of fate within the play in terms of: the contemporary Jacobean debate between Calvinistic predestination and the alternative Arminian view of salvation being achievable through free will (**AO3**); the synthesis of fate and the will of the gods as found in the tragedies of Ancient Greece and Rome (**AO3**); Webster's use of meta-theatrical language and parallel scenes to suggest the workings of a greater power, as well as a universal synchronicity (**AO1/AO2**); the characters' various references to fate (**AO2**); and the play's characteristic 'revenge tragedy' denouement in which retribution for evil is framed in terms of Christian ethics (**AO3**). The student supports all of this via a sustained analysis of textual examples (**AO1**).

If the rest of the student's answer reached a similar level to the extract, it would be likely to receive a Grade A.

Developing and linking: go with the flow

An essay is a very specific type of formal writing, which requires an appropriate discourse structure. In the main body of your writing, you need to thread your developing argument through each paragraph consistently and logically, referring back to the terms established by the question itself, rephrasing and reframing as you go. It can be challenging to sustain the flow of your essay and keep firmly on track, but here are some techniques to help you:

▼ Ensure your essay doesn't disintegrate into a series of disconnected building blocks by creating a neat and stable bridge between each paragraph and the next.

▼ Use discourse markers – linking words and phrases like *on the other hand*, *however*, *although* and *moreover* – to hold the individual paragraphs of your essay together and to signpost the connections between different sections of your overarching argument.

▼ Having set out an idea in Paragraph A, in Paragraph B you might then need to support it by providing a further example; if so, signal this to the reader with a phrase such as **Moreover,** *this use of light and dark imagery can also be seen when…*

▼ To change direction and challenge an idea begun in Paragraph A by acknowledging that it is open to interpretation, you could begin Paragraph B with something like **On the other hand,** *this view of the play could be challenged by a feminist critic…*

▼ Another typical paragraph-to-paragraph link is when you want to show that the original idea doesn't give the full picture. Here you could modify your original point with something like **Although** *it is possible to see the First Pilgrim's remarks about Antonio as snobbish and elitist, this view does not take account of the social context of the early Jacobean period when such comments would have been the norm.*

Student B

The following paragraphs are from the middle section of Student B's response to the same Edexcel A-level exam-style question:

Explore the presentation of fate in *The Duchess of Malfi*. You must relate your discussion to relevant contextual factors.

…Thus all of the main characters seem to be affected by 'fate' and 'the stars'.

Perhaps the best example to begin with is the Duchess herself as she is the protagonist. In Act IV scene 1 after Ferdinand and Bosola have convinced her that Antonio and their children are dead, she angrily says to Bosola 'I could curse the stars.' She is clearly depressed just as Ferdinand wanted her to be and is now expressing a desire to die. Webster does ensure, however, that she mentally recovers just before her eventual execution and so he keeps her as a tragic heroine.

When the Duchess refers to the 'stars' this is a reference to fate, which in revenge tragedy is generally seen to be a hostile force. When in Act III scene 5, however, Webster has the Duchess declare 'Oh heaven, thy heavy hand is in 't!' he is also showing the power of God to influence the future and so it could be that fate and God's will are the same thing.

Examiner's commentary

This student:

- offers a clearly written response with good SPaG (**A01**)
- uses relevant textual examples, but not perhaps always well assimilated or embedded in the point they are making (**A01**)
- uses relevant subject terminology and concepts (**A01**)
- shows some appreciation of Webster's craft and the ways in which he creates meaning (**A02**)
- makes an excellent observation on the relationship between fate and God, if somewhat simplistically expressed. An A/A*candidate might have introduced a critical perspective here, e.g. by referencing Aristotle's *Poetics*. Aristotle indicates that fate and the will of the gods are indistinguishable in ancient Greek drama as the gods seek to punish the hero for his hamartia, his 'error of judgement or frailty', especially hubris (pride) (**A03**)
- goes off-topic when discussing the Duchess' despair (**A01**)
- misses the opportunity to discuss the Duchess' specific 'error of judgement or frailty' – her young woman's desire for love – as a determining factor in her own destiny (**A01**).

This student's performance remains consistent throughout the rest of the essay. It is not a top-band response, however, because of the occasional drifting off-topic. Also, unlike Student A, this student did not think to explore the contrary interpretation of the possible exertion of free will within the play. Examples of this could include the series of choices that Bosola makes that ultimately result in the deaths of all the major characters including himself, or Webster's presentation of powerful societal forces that dictate events (**A03**).

If the rest of the student's answer reached a similar level of performance, it would be likely to gain a Grade C.

Concluding: seal the deal

As you bring your writing to a close, you need to capture and clarify your response to the given view and make a relatively swift and elegant exit. Keep your final paragraph short and sweet. Now is not the time to introduce any new points – but equally, don't simply reword everything you have already just said either. Neat potential closers include:

- ◤ Looping the last paragraph back to something you mentioned in your introduction to suggest that you have now said all there is to say on the subject.
- ◤ Reflecting on your key points in order to reach a balanced overview.
- ◤ Ending with a punchy quotation that leaves the reader thinking.
- ◤ Discussing the contextual implications of the topic you have debated.
- ◤ Reversing expectations to end on an interesting alternative view.
- ◤ Stating why you think the main issue, theme or character under discussion is so central to the play.
- ◤ Mentioning how different audiences over time might have responded to the topic you have been debating.

Student C

This conclusion from a student response is in answer to the same Edexcel A-level exam-style question:

Explore the presentation of fate in *The Duchess of Malfi*. You must relate your discussion to relevant contextual factors.

In Act V, all of the major characters meet their fate: the Duchess is already dead, Bosola accidentally kills Antonio, Bosola kills the Cardinal and Ferdinand, and Ferdinand kills Bosola. A Jacobean audience would see this as justice for all the evil that has been committed, although many would feel sympathy for the Duchess and Antonio. They were good characters and so did not deserve what happened to them, although they did defy social convention when they married in secret against the Duchess' brothers' wishes. Also, the fact that they are from different social classes would have been frowned on by many in the audience of Webster's time because of the belief in the Great Chain of Being. Modern audiences would be much more sympathetic, though, especially Marxist and feminist critics, who would point out the rigid nature of Jacobean society and the way it discriminated against women and the middle and lower classes.

Examiner's commentary

This student:

- ❯ appears to view fate only from the narrow perspective of signifying God's punishment (**A01**)

- ❯ fails to conclude effectively as it does not focus in upon the original task or clarify the main argument of the essay (**A01**)

- ❯ drifts off-topic to a consideration of other issues that have only been very loosely related to the main topic (**A01**)

- ❯ there is, however, an astute appreciation of how the impact of the play has changed over time (**A03**), but the student makes a serious mistake by referring to genres of literary criticism and how they can foster different interpretations, as A05 is not assessed in this part of the exam for Edexcel.

- ❯ some relevant, if very general, conclusions have been made regarding the possible workings of fate within the play (**A01/A02**).

In the sections that preceded this conclusion, the student did explore in some detail the main characters' various references to fate and how Webster thus presented them as if they believed in fate as the prime mover in their affairs. There was no discussion, however, of whether the characters were representing Webster's views in this respect, nor was there any real consideration of what else 'fate' could mean, beyond the will of God.

Overall, the candidate is likely to have shown sufficient understanding of both the question and the text just to gain Grade C.

Building skills 2: Analysing texts in detail

Having worked through the previous section on structuring your writing, this section of the guide contains a range of annotated extracts from students' responses to *The Duchess of Malfi.* The next few pages will enable you to assess the extent to which these students have successfully demonstrated their writing skills and mastery of the Assessment Objectives. This will provide you with an index by which to measure your own skills progress. Each extract comes with a commentary to help you identify what each student is doing well and/or what changes they would need to make to their writing to target a higher grade.

The main focus here is on the ways in which you can successfully include within your own well-structured writing clear and appropriate references to both *The Duchess of Malfi* itself and to the ways in which other readers have responded to the play.

Student D

This student is answering a WJEC Eduqas or OCR exam-style question that proposes a specific view. The comparative text for WJEC Eduqas is *A Streetcar Named Desire*. For OCR, the comparison would be between *The Duchess of Malfi* and a poetry text. The question, which is clearly designed to open up a debate, is:

'The tragic imagination is essentially a moral one, though by no means a moralising one.' In light of this statement, explore connections between *The Duchess of Malfi* and *A Streetcar Named Desire*.

The critic Northrop Frye expresses an opposing view to the above statement when he suggests that when tragedy is written to provide a moral message, it begins to lose its cathartic power. Frye's reference to catharsis is based on Aristotle's analysis of tragedy as an emotionally engaging and rejuvenating experience for the audience. If Frye is correct, then tragedy loses its ability to provide this emotional release for its audience the more it attempts to promote a moral cause. And yet in agreement with the opening statement, both Webster and Williams powerfully engage our sympathies for their tragic heroines exactly by appalling us with the senseless cruelty that is inflicted upon them. Thus the tragic imagination of both of these great dramatists is 'essentially a moral one'. The main difference, however, is that Webster is far more explicitly didactic in pointing out the errors of his characters' ways.

The reason for this difference in approach is historical and cultural. Webster was writing at a time and in a society when the Bible was the most important text and thus it would have been far more acceptable for him to openly moralise than it would have been for Williams, who was writing in the twentieth century when the outlook was far more secular (although Williams was born in Mississippi, which is in the USA's Bible Belt). Furthermore, Webster, like all of the other great English Renaissance dramatists, was heavily influenced by the Classical literature of Ancient Greece and Rome, especially Senecan drama, which also frequently provided direct moral instruction through use of the Chorus. Thus in the play's closing lines, Webster uses Delio as an explicitly didactic moralising choric voice when he has him declare that the 'Integrity of life is fame's best friend...'

Student E

This student is also answering a WJEC Eduqas- or OCR-type question. The question, which is clearly designed to open up a debate, is:

'The ode lives upon the ideal, the epic upon the grandiose, the drama upon the real.'

How far would you agree that Webster and Williams are alike in dramatising 'the real' in *The Duchess of Malfi* and *A Streetcar Named Desire*?

In 'The Duchess of Malfi' and 'A Streetcar Named Desire' both dramatists do attempt to deal with what is real, although Williams is more real than Webster because he sets his play in the real world of his audience and not in some remote Italian setting a hundred years beforehand, as Webster does. Also, Williams writes about real people with real problems – people we might meet every day – whereas Webster writes about duchesses and dukes. What Webster writes about is so far removed from reality that it really does not have much to say to the ordinary man in the street. So, for example, we are presented with a brother who is a nobleman, has sexual fantasies about his twin sister and thinks he is a werewolf!

Another problem with 'The Duchess of Malfi' is the dumb show in Act III and the antimasque of the madmen in Act IV. Webster uses artificial ways of presenting his themes, whereas Williams presents lifelike domestic situations and uses recognisable everyday dialogue. Webster, on the other hand, writes in blank verse and rhyming couplets called sententiae. But my biggest issue with Webster is definitely the characterisation. Not only is Ferdinand stark mad and Bosola irredeemably evil but Antonio, unlike Stanley Kowalski, is a proper wimp!

Examiner's commentary

This student:

- directly attempts to handle the debate and define what 'real' means, although rather simplistically (**A01**)
- makes a valiant attempt to compare the plays (**A04**)
- is very aware that Webster and Williams are the makers of textual meaning (**A02**) (A02 is not examined by OCR for *The Duchess of Malfi*)
- shows some awareness of how the dramatic conventions of Jacobean drama help to differentiate it from modern drama (**A03**)
- doesn't really address **A03** with any real conviction, however, because it requires that you 'Demonstrate understanding of the significance and influence of the contexts in which literary texts are written and received'; consequently, he/she fails to appreciate that much of what might seem 'unreal' today, such as Ferdinand's lycanthropia, was considered 'real' in Jacobean society
- as a result, the consideration of the opening premise is rather simplistic (**A05**)
- also fails to realise that the Italian court was a convenient mechanism by which Jacobean dramatists addressed English political issues and that Antonio's perceived passivity had very much been predetermined for him by the rigid class structure of the time (**A03**)
- furthermore, fails to realise that most great drama is unreal in the sense that it is heightened reality and thus most of us do not, as the student suggests, encounter households as dysfunctional as the Kowalskis' every day (**A01**)

Despite its obvious flaws, there is a considerable degree of critical awareness demonstrated here. If the rest of the examination answer attained this level of performance, it is likely the student would be on course to achieve a Grade C.

Extended commentaries

In every kind of essay you will need to demonstrate your ability to analyse the way in which authors use language and form to create and shape meaning. You should practise this by writing analyses of particular passages from the text. This will have the added benefit of encouraging you to explore the text further, and will generate ideas that you can utilise in any essay you need to write.

Examples of such analyses are given below.

Extended commentary 1

Appearance and reality in Act III scene 2, lines 255–310 ('But he was basely descended' to 'Sir, your direction / Shall lead me by the hand').

In his article 'The function of imagery in Webster' (1955), Hereward T. Price claims that 'Webster especially uses imagery to convey the basic conflict of his drama, the conflict between outward appearance and inner substance or reality'. Price goes on to define this as evil attempting to present itself as 'pure gold', whereas 'good tries to protect itself by putting on disguise or a false show'. As in all English Renaissance tragedy, this invariably precipitates disaster, usually because a hero is secretly attempting to transgress a moral or social code or because a villain is surreptitiously intent on orchestrating the hero's demise, an excellent example being Iago in Shakespeare's 'Othello'. In this pivotal extract from *The Duchess of Malfi*, we have both strands of the appearance–reality dichotomy simultaneously in play.

At the beginning of the extract, the Duchess is still busily engaged in perpetuating the deception that Antonio is her steward, to which she has added the subterfuge that she has just dismissed him for embezzlement. This is merely a ruse, however, in order to expedite the family's departure from court owing to Ferdinand's discovery that Antonio is in fact her husband. The Duchess thus uses deception in order to protect herself by continuing to conceal her social transgression.

Bosola, too, has long practised a deception upon the Duchess, pretending to be her Provisor of the Horse when, in fact, his real employment is as a spy for her brothers. Whereas she now abandons her deception, he continues with his, embarking upon a deceit which is truly villainous. Having tricked her into revealing the <u>reality</u> of her situation by <u>appearing</u> to be sympathetic towards Antonio, he pretends to give her good advice with regard to her escape while secretly plotting her entrapment.

The appearance-reality dichotomy deepens even more when Webster skilfully begins to envelop the audience in the web of misconception. Bosola's praise of Antonio and his further extolling of the Duchess' meritocratic choice of a husband for his virtue and not his social position, draws forth from him the enthusiastic vision of 'an ambitious age'. Bosola asks if it is possible that the world is finally free of 'these shadows / Of wealth and painted honours?'

Bosola's metaphors advance Webster's theme by pointing out the discrepancy between what society regards as noble and what is genuinely noble in terms of morality. According to Bosola, society's conceptions of honour are merely surface-deep appearances, being 'painted' and no more substantial than 'shadows'. To add further ambiguity, Bosola is asking a question rather than making a statement. But the real dilemma for the audience is whether, when Bosola extols the Duchess' meritocratic choice, it is just a pretence or actually a deeply held conviction? After all, on other occasions he cites his own lack of opportunity as one of the main springs for his immoral behaviour: 'Say then my corruption / Grew out of horse dung.'

Ultimately, though, Bosola, the arch-deceiver and weaver of so many false realities for the hapless Duchess (especially after he discovers her secret in the climactic moment in the appearance-reality motif), is himself equally deceived and mystified about the true reality of his own existence. As he implies shortly before his death in Act V, he has lived his life 'in a mist'. Unlike Bosola's, Webster's own vision of life is crystal clear, however, and it is one that is finally imparted to Bosola in his final breath: the certainty of 'another voyage', that being a voyage to hell, a divine retribution for a sinful life. Of course, at the close of this extract, Bosola is as morally blind as ever and clearly living under the delusion that he is master of his own fate as he blithely begins the process of conducting the Duchess through an intricate web of deceit that ultimately ends with her death … and his damnation.

Extended commentary 2

The Duchess' death scene, Act IV scene 2, lines 199–223 ('Yet, methinks, / The manner of your death should much afflict you…' to 'They strangle her').

This is arguably the play's emotional climax as it portrays, in graphic detail, the death of the tragic heroine. Webster, though, breaks with the English Renaissance dramatic convention by staging it at the end of the fourth act rather than at the end of the fifth. In order to maximise the emotional impact, however, he does closely follow other established aesthetic traditions that were prevalent at the time. These are, firstly, the Aristotelian concept that a tragic hero should be a recognisably human character of social eminence, who should receive a punishment that greatly exceeds their hamartia, i.e. their 'error of judgement or frailty'; secondly, the Classical pagan tradition of stoicism; and thirdly, the *ars moriendi,* a body of Christian literature that emphasised dying well in order to achieve salvation. Having created a character who has continually been shown to be both human and fallible, in this extract Webster has the Duchess rise to tragic heroism, and Christian martyrdom, through the courage and equanimity she displays in the face of Bosola's malicious attempt to terrify her by displaying the rope with which she will be strangled.

One of the main causes of the controversy created by Webster's work is the seeming impotence of good in the face of evil, which has caused critics such as

Travis Bogard to view Webster's work as essentially nihilistic, presenting only 'moral chaos'. For Bogard, Webster's work depicts a universe that is ultimately pointless: 'Death is clearly the end ... Man, after a few years of struggle, comes to nothing. Whatever his degree of magnificence, whether he adhered to the traditional principles of good or indulged in bizarre evils, he comes inevitably to dust. And the dust has no meaning.' (*The Tragic Satire of John Webster*, 1955). Irving Ribner, however, has a much more positive view of Webster's vision, especially as it is exemplified in this extract, when he declares 'Into it comes the Duchess of Malfi who stands for the values of life, and Webster's final statement is that life may have nobility in spite of all' (*Jacobean Tragedy: The Quest for Moral Order*, 1962).

To my mind, however, Webster's vision is neither nihilistic nor just one of life-affirming exemplars like the Duchess. As Lord David Cecil states in *Poets and Storytellers* (1949), Webster dramatises 'the battle of heaven and hell' and thus his is a deeply moral vision which, like Shakespeare, Ford and other notable contemporaries, clearly views the universe in terms of the polar absolutes of Good and Evil. This comes out most powerfully in this extract through Webster's presentation of the Duchess' unshakeable faith, which is reinforced through both her actions and her words. Thus, although a high-born woman – 'I am Duchess of Malfi still' as she defiantly declares earlier in the scene – she has not lost sight of her essential humanity. In an act of extreme humility, she kneels before God with every expectation of subsequently entering through 'heaven gates'.

Many critics, especially A.C. Swinburne, have drawn attention to the power of Webster's poetry; in *The Age of Shakespeare* (1908) he extols Webster's 'Mere literary power, mere poetic beauty'. One of the ways in which Webster makes the Duchess' death experience so vivid and moving is through the use of highly original imagery, which startlingly concretises the abstract. Consequently, the Duchess' transition from Earth to heaven is made intensely vivid through the physicality of the metaphor that suggests heaven can be pulled down upon her. Similarly, Webster provides a strikingly fresh perspective on death by making it appear both tangible and chillingly close at hand! The Duchess informs us that it 'hath ten thousand several doors' and that it has 'geometrical hinges', which 'open ... both ways'. This presents death as a trap that attempts to ensnare us at every turn and that is impossible to avoid or outmanoeuvre. In this way, Webster proves Swinburne's further analysis that his poetry gives remarkable expression to universal truth. Consequently, 'thus and not otherwise it must have been'.

Before studying this section, you should identify your own 'top ten' quotations – i.e. those phrases or sentences that capture a key theme, aspect of symbolism or character most aptly and memorably – and identify clearly what it is about your choices that makes each one so significant. No two readers of *The Duchess of Malfi* will select exactly the same set and it will be well worth discussing (and perhaps even having to defend) your choices with the other students in your class.

When you have done this, look carefully at the following list of ten quotations and consider each one's significance within the play. How might each be used in an essay response to support your exploration of various elements or readings of *The Duchess of Malfi*? Consider what these quotations tell us about Webster's ideas, themes and methods, as well as how far they may contribute to various potential ways of interpreting the text.

1 '…but if 't chance / Some cursed example poison 't near the head, / Death and diseases through the whole land spread.' (Antonio, I.1)

⊣ Structurally, this is important as it clearly signals to the audience from the very start what the play is going to be about: how corrupt rule will of necessity lead to corruption throughout the state, an idea reiterated throughout the play. The metaphor is extended a little later on in Act I when Bosola refers to the court in terms of 'standing pools', i.e. stagnant water that is generally a breeding ground for bacteria and parasites.

2 'This goodly roof of yours is too low built, / …Raise yourself, / Or if you please, my hand to help you: so.' (Duchess to Antonio, I.1)

⊣ Again, a metaphor is used to introduce and illustrate an important aspect of the rigid hierarchical structure of this society, one that mirrors Webster's own view in terms of its value systems. Antonio is noble in bearing, thought and action, but he is inferior by birth. The Duchess, in choosing to marry him, is 'raising him up' into her social sphere. At this point in the play, Antonio is kneeling in humility before his 'Prince', the Duchess, and Webster here plays on his audience's visual and auditory senses in giving us dialogue to match the corresponding action, in order to reinforce the precise nature of the Duchess' rebellion against the dictates of her social order. Coming immediately after the scene where her aristocratic brothers have forbidden her to remarry, let alone to a commoner, Webster builds tension and raises questions about the wisdom of the Duchess as well as the fitness of such a social order, another idea echoed throughout the play. The quotation is also significant in that it perfectly reflects the touching sensitivity with which Webster writes this love scene.

'The great are like the base, nay, they are the same, / When they seek shameful ways to avoid shame.' (Antonio, II.3)

3

- This is one of the many sententiae that appear in the play, often rounding off a speech before the exit of a character in order to leave the audience with a short space to digest and ponder what is meant to be a fundamental truth. Webster highlights Antonio's discomfort, voiced elsewhere by the Duchess, with the fact that they must hide their union under a cloak of deceit as if they have done something shameworthy in defying class boundaries in order to love and marry one another. The sententia suggests that these class boundaries are artificial as everybody shares a common humanity. It also helps to advance the important appearance and reality theme that was so predominant in English Renaissance drama.

'Shall our blood, / The royal blood of Aragon and Castile, / Be thus attainted?' (Cardinal to Ferdinand, II.5)

4

- In characteristically cold and dispassionate terms, the Cardinal expresses the notion that his aristocratic blood will be contaminated by the Duchess' union with a commoner. This speech clearly portrays the depth of outrage with which many in Jacobean society would view such a socially unequal marriage.

'Why might not I marry? / I have not gone about in this to create / Any new world or custom.' (Duchess, III.2)

5

- And yet that is exactly what she has done. Her marriage to Antonio is a clear challenge to the established social order but she is too spiritual, free from prejudice and, possibly, naive to see it.

'Oh misery, methinks unjust actions / Should wear these masks and curtains, and not we…' (Duchess, III.2)

6

- As with Antonio's words in Quotation 3, Webster uses the Duchess to reflect the distorted status quo through the idea of the good having to stoop to deceit to protect themselves from the bad, while the latter seem, in the present order of the world, far freer to pursue their ends in the open. Again Webster appears to be profoundly questioning Jacobean society both in terms of its rigid class lines and its patriarchal structure. The metaphor is also part of the powerful appearance–reality motif.

7 'The birds that live i'th'field / ...live / Happier than we; for they may choose their mates / And carol their sweet pleasures to the spring.' (Duchess, III.5)

 ▾ Webster highlights the unnaturalness of a society in which marriages are made for political and material gain, and in which love is a secondary consideration. The bird imagery suggests that marriage should be predicated on natural instinct, pure motive and a desire for mutual fulfilment. It also expresses a powerful desire for freedom.

8 'Pray thee, why dost thou wrap thy poisoned pills / In gold and sugar?' (Duchess to Bosola, IV.1)

 ▾ Central to the metaphor are the two big recurring motifs of poison or corruption, and of appearance and reality, in which disguise is so often used to mask evil.

9 'We are merely the stars' tennis balls, struck and banded / Which way please them.' (Bosola, V.4)

 ▾ Bosola states this after accidentally killing Antonio. The metaphor reflects the Classical motif of a seemingly malevolent fate as a prime mover in human affairs but, as in the tradition of the drama of Ancient Greece and Rome, it is difficult to draw a dividing line between fate and the will of God. Furthermore, at the time when Webster was writing, Calvinism was a predominant Protestant creed, with its emphasis on predestination in which an elite group, 'the elect', would ascend to heaven while the rest are fated to hell. Bosola is clearly not one of the elect and through Antonio's accidental slaying Webster ensures that he will fail in his efforts to find redemption.

10 'Let us make noble use / Of this great ruin; and join all our force / To establish this young hopeful gentleman / In's mother's right.' (Delio, V.5)

 ▾ The final speech of the play, given to a member of the ruling class, reinforces that positive social change can only be initiated from within the ruling class. Why? Because outside of the aristocracy, as Webster has shown us throughout his play, there is insufficient power to initiate anything, which is most likely the reason why Antonio continually appears as weak and ineffective. There is also irony here, however, as although some might interpret this as a hopeful ending, others might remember the horoscope made earlier in the play for this same child, which predicted an early and violent death. The ending thus perpetuates what many critics view as the play's moral ambiguity by helping to fuel the debate as to whether Webster's message is primarily one of spiritual optimism or nihilistic despair.

Appendix

William Painter's *Duchess of Malfy* as recounted in *The Palace of Pleasure*, Volume 3

Giovanna d'Aragona, the real Duchess of Malfi, was born in 1478 and, as her father had died of poisoning before her birth, would have been under the control of her brothers. She was married in 1490 when she was only twelve years old. Her first husband became the Duke of Amalfi after his own father's death in 1493, but then died himself in 1498. Historically, the majority of the events that take place in the play actually occurred between 1508 and 1513. The timeframe that Webster uses for his play is slightly different; it probably begins in early 1504 and ends approximately three or four years later.

Although accounts of Giovanna's tragedy appeared in various forms, Webster's drama appears to have been mainly modelled on the version that appeared in Volume 3 of William Painter's *The Palace of Pleasure*, which was published in the late 1560s. Painter's translation of earlier 'Italian and French novels' is a re-telling of a true story that was originally told by Matteo Bandello in his *Novelle* (1554). Webster's heavy borrowing from Painter should not, however, in any way be seen as undermining the play's integrity as a great work of literature, nor Webster's status as a great dramatist. Such adaption was extremely common among the playwrights of the age, including Shakespeare.

Painter's story begins with a detailed description of Antonio Bologna, a valiant soldier, skilled horseman and talented musician, who is also extremely handsome and athletically built. He had served as Master of the Household to the former King of Naples now exiled to France, Frederick of Aragon. Having heard of what an honest and able administrator he was to Frederick, the Duchess of Malfi entreats him to run her affairs in a likewise manner.

As a result of her husband's premature death, the beautiful young widow has inherited the Italian city-state of Malfi, which she now rules as regent until her infant son becomes of age. At this point, Painter provides an incredibly sympathetic portrait of a young woman who longs for the love and physical intimacy she had known when her husband was alive. Thus, she soon becomes infatuated with Antonio. Of course, she is acutely aware of the difference in their social status but reasons to herself that she is free to marry and, fundamentally, there is no real difference between aristocrats and commoners as they all share a common humanity.

She explains to Antonio that since her husband's death, she has ably administered her lands. She has paid all of the former Duke's debts and prospered sufficiently well to annex the state of Ancona. She explains to him that she wishes to marry and intends to choose a husband who is virtuous rather than one who is rich. She reveals that her brothers will be infuriated by any such marriage, especially the Cardinal, and thus for the safety of both herself and her husband, the marriage will have to be kept secret. The Duchess is well aware that Antonio feels a similar passion for her and so she takes his hand and proposes to him. Despite his concerns regarding the difference in their social status, and his fear of retribution from her brothers, his love for her is so great that he accepts. He also reasons away his fears by convincing himself that they will be able to reconcile the two brothers to the marriage. The following day they are secretly married in her chamber, with just the Duchess' gentlewoman – brought up with her from birth – as a witness.

Although the birth of their first child, a boy, is kept secret, the birth of their second child, a girl, becomes common gossip. The gossip spreads throughout Italy and eventually reaches her brother, the Cardinal of Aragon, who resides in Rome. Both of the Duchess' brothers are furious at such a corruption of their family blood but determine not to act until they have discovered the identity of the father, and thus they employ spies to work inside the Duchess' court in order to help them enact their revenge. Antonio, fearing discovery of their dangerous secret, and even at one point erroneously suspecting the loyalty of the Duchess' faithful gentlewoman, moves himself and their two children to Naples so as to lessen the chances of discovery. His intention is to order his affairs and then proceed to Ancona in order to mitigate the rage of the brothers. The Duchess, now pregnant with their third child, reluctantly agrees to the plan.

As the Duchess' pregnancy advances, she lives in greater fear of discovery and longs to be reunited with her husband and their two children. Her waiting woman's advice is to use the pretext of a pilgrimage to the Holy Temple of Our Lady of Loreto in order to escape Malfi and its many spies. The Duchess willingly agrees to the plan, despite the fact that she will lose her title and her lands by doing so and must leave behind her son by her first marriage. By this stage of the story, Painter has clearly lost all of his apparent original sympathy for the Duchess, calling her a 'foolish woman' and condemning her for marrying below her status. He also reproaches her for her feigned pilgrimage.

Having visited Loreto, the Duchess and her party immediately proceed to join Antonio in Ancona where, the day after her arrival, she announces to all of their servants that Antonio is her husband and the father of their three children. Apart from her faithful waiting woman, all the other servants take up her offer to leave her service and return to Malfi to serve the young Duke by her first marriage and, out of fear of the Cardinal, one of them is sent to Rome to inform him of the news. Although the Cardinal is incensed, it is the younger brother who expresses the most outrage, calling the Duchess 'a false and vile bytch', referring to her 'whorish heate' and threatening a terrible revenge.

The Cardinal immediately uses his influence in order to have the Duchess, Antonio and their family exiled from Ancona, as the two brothers hope to enact a bloody revenge once the lovers have left the safety of the city. Antonio arranges to flee to Siena with his family. They arrive there safely much to the chagrin of the brothers. The brothers then use their influence, via Alfonso Castruccio, the Cardinal of Siena, to persuade the authorities to have the family yet again banished, causing them to flee this time to Venice.

While in transit, the party is overtaken by a troupe of horsemen. The Duchess persuades a reluctant Antonio to flee on horseback with their eldest son as there is no hope of escape for any of the others in their party, whereupon he and his son make their way to Milan.

One of the horsemen who has waylaid the party expresses his amazement that the Duchess should have married 'a man of so smal reputation as Bologna is' and then accuses the departed Antonio of being a coward. The Duchess and what remains of her group are to be returned to Malfi, as commanded by her two brothers, where she will resume her former status. Rather than being safely returned to Malfi as promised, however, they are taken to Naples and imprisoned. Some days after her imprisonment, she is visited by a gaoler who informs her that she is to be executed that day.

Painter describes the Duchess' anguish as she torments herself with the question of why her marriage should be treated the same as great crimes such as murder, theft and adultery. She also questions the Cardinal's Christianity and then humbly begs forgiveness from God for whatever sins she has committed. The Duchess pleads with the ministers who come briefly to prepare her for death to protect her two babies and her waiting woman. The ministers promise to do as she has asked and she is then strangled by 'two ruffians'. The Duchess thus dies with great courage and dignity. The ministers now ignore the Duchess' last wishes and the ruffians next kill the waiting woman for having been complicit in the Duchess' secret personal life. Finally, the Duchess' two infant children beg for mercy but they too are dispatched. Painter makes clear that all of this was done on the orders of the Duchess' brothers.

Meanwhile, Antonio is still in Milan with his eldest son. Agents of the two brothers tell him that the stories he has heard of the Duchess' death are untrue and that her two brothers intend to be reconciled with him. Encouraged by the hope this gives him, he remains in Milan for a period of more than a year. One day a stranger called Delio approaches Antonio and says that, being a virtuous man himself, he recognises the same quality in Antonio. He warns Antonio that he has been informed by a captain that the Duchess and her children have been murdered and that her brothers have commissioned Antonio's assassination. Antonio refuses to believe the story and claims that Delio has been deceived. He says that in the past two days he has received letters from the Aragonian brothers that state both his property and his wife will be returned to him. Delio warns Antonio that the letters are false and are part of a shameful plot to murder him.

Painter then describes the man who has been paid to be Antonio's assassin, a 'bloudy beaste' called Daniel de Bozola. He and a troupe of soldiers murder Antonio as he leaves church. Painter informs us that the Cardinal had also commissioned the assassination of a perfectly innocent man many years before, though there is no suggestion that Bozola was the assassin.

Painter concludes by re-emphasising the moral of the tale: 'You see the miserable discourse of a Princesse loue, that was not very wyse, and of a Gentleman that had forgotten his estate'. The Duchess' unwise passion for a commoner and Antonio's failure to keep in his allotted social position are therefore seen as the main causes of the tragedy.

Taking it further

Painter's *Duchess of Malfy*

❧ The full text of William Painter's *Duchess of Malfy* can be found at:
www.gutenberg.org/files/34840/34840-h/34840-h.htm#contents

Editions of the play

❧ Gibbons, Brian (ed.) *The Duchess of Malfi*, New Mermaids (2014) – contains an excellent introduction and editorial notes.

❧ Gunby, David (ed.) *John Webster: Three Plays*, The Penguin English Library (1972) – contains an excellent introduction about Webster and the critical debate he arouses.

Criticism

❧ Fox, Timothy *A Discussion of Morality and Horror in* The Duchess of Malfi *and* Edward II (2002) – an interesting contribution to the debate regarding whether Webster's work contains any meaningful moral intent – available online at www.luminarium.org/sevenlit/foxwebster.htm

❧ Gosse, Edmund *The Jacobean Poets* (1894) – Chapter 8 provides a fascinating Victorian perspective on Webster's perceived strengths and weaknesses. Gosse's entire text is available online at: https://archive.org/details/jacobeanpoets01gossgoog

❧ Jack, Ian 'The Case of John Webster', in *Scrutiny* (1949) – one of the most hostile reviews of Webster's work, which is most definitely a fascinating read and is available online at: www.unz.org/Pub/Scrutiny-1949mar-00038

❧ Salingar, L.G. 'The Elizabethan Literary Renaissance', in B. Ford (ed.) *The Pelican Guide to English Literature, Volume 2: The Age of Shakespeare* (1963)
Salingar, L.G. 'The Social Setting', in B. Ford (ed.) *The Pelican Guide to English Literature, Volume 2: The Age of Shakespeare* (1963)
Salingar, L.G. 'Tourneur and the Tragedy of Revenge', in B. Ford (ed.) *The Pelican Guide to English Literature, Volume 2: The Age of Shakespeare* (1963)
– all three chapters are excellent for an understanding of the historical context.

Websites

❧ www.open.edu/openlearn/history-the-arts/culture/literature-and-creative-writing/literature/john-webster-the-duchess-malfi/content-section-0 – an analysis of Acts I and II of *The Duchess of Malfi* by the Open University.

NB: the relevant Open University pages can best be accessed by pasting the hyperlink into Google: if you simply put the link into your address bar, it will not pull up the relevant pages.

- ❐ www.shmoop.com/the-duchess-of-malfi – contains extremely detailed scene summaries as well as humorous analyses of many aspects of the play.
- ❐ https://en.wikipedia.org/wiki/The_Duchess_of_Malfi – a most useful and informative analysis of many aspects of the play.
- ❐ www.bbc.co.uk/programmes/articles/2nF1ZyFkQ1q8RdSvrYYbZDW/the-duchess-of-malfi – a series of useful articles about both Webster and *The Duchess of Malfi* written to accompany Dominic Dromgoole's 2014 production of the play starring Gemma Arterton, plus links to selected scenes from this production.
- ❐ www.bbc.co.uk/education/guides/z2wp34j/revision/3 – provides excellent information in a very readable form about the audience and social attitudes in Shakespearean England.

Audiovisual resources

- ❐ The 1972 BBC production of the play, directed by James MacTaggart, is available on YouTube.
- ❐ An excellent 2010 stage production of the play is available on DVD from www.stageonscreen.com